THREE MEN

Three Men in a Jeep Called "Ma Kabul"
Script for a Movie

A True Story of High Adventure by
Three Allied Intelligence Officers in World War II

By

George J. Hill, M.D., D.Litt.
Captain, Medical Corps, USNR (ret)

HERITAGE BOOKS
2018

HERITAGE BOOKS
AN IMPRINT OF HERITAGE BOOKS, INC.

Books, CDs, and more—Worldwide

For our listing of thousands of titles see our website
at
www.HeritageBooks.com

Published 2018 by
HERITAGE BOOKS, INC.
Publishing Division
5810 Ruatan Street
Berwyn Heights, Md. 20740

Copyright © 2018 George J. Hill, M.D., M.A., D.Litt.

Heritage Books by the author:
*American Dreams: Ancestors and Descendants of John Zimmerman and
Eva Katherine Kellenbenz Who Were Married in Philadelphia in 1885
"Dearest Barb" from Karachi, 1943-1945: Letters and Photographs in the World War II Papers
of a Naval Intelligence Officer, Lieutenant Albert Zimmermann, USNR
Edison's Environment: Invention and Pollution in the Career of Thomas Edison
Four Families: A Tetralogy. Readers Guide to Western Pilgrims,
Quakers and Puritans, Fundy to Chesapeake, and American Dreams
Fundy to Chesapeake: The Thompson, Rundall and Allied Families. Ancestors and Descendants of
William Henry Thompson and Sarah D. Rundall, Who Were Married in Linn County, Iowa, in 1889
Hill: The Ferry Keeper's Family. Luke Hill and Mary Hout, Who were Married in Windsor, Connecticut, in 1651
and Fourteen Generations of Their Known and Possible Descendants
John Saxe, Loyalist (1732–1808) and His Descendants for Five Generations
Quakers and Puritans: The Shoemaker, Warren and Allied Families. Ancestors and Descendants of
William Toy Shoemaker and Mabel Warren, Who Were Married in Philadelphia in 1895
Western Pilgrims: The Hill, Stockwell and Allied Families. Ancestors and Descendants of George J. Hill
and Jessie Fidelia Stockwell, Who Were Married in Wright County, Iowa, in 1882*

Illustrations

Most of the photos and stills from movies are from the Wartime Papers of Albert Zimmermann. Some were previously published by the U.S. Naval Institute Press. Others were previously published by Heritage Books. All of the photos and original movies are now in Zimmermann's Papers in Special Collections at the U.S. Naval Institute. Other photos are from Google Images.

Cover designed by Debbie Riley

All rights reserved. No part of this book may be reproduced or transmitted in any form or by any means, electronic or mechanical, including photocopying, recording or by any information storage and retrieval system without written permission from the author, except for the inclusion of brief quotations in a review.

International Standard Book Numbers
Paperbound:
Clothbound:

Dedicated to the Memory of
The Three Men

Lieutenant Albert Zimmermann on Lowari Pass
Afghanistan is in the background

Major Sir Benjamin Bromhead and Major Gordon Enders
in Waziristan

And their jeep, called "Ma Kabul"

Contents

Frontispiece – The Jeep, "Ma Kabul," with Major Enders at the wheel	v
Dedication to the Three Men	vi
Contents	vii
Preface	viii
Prologue	xi
Log Line and Pitch	1
Introduction	3
Scenario for the Script	7
The Script	11
Scenario for the Trailer	125
The Trailer	127
Post Script Notes and Sample Illustrations	137
Still Shots from Zimmermann's Films	147
Acknowledgements	155
Bibliography	157
Other Books by the Author	163
About the Author	164

Preface

Would you like to make a movie? A documentary? Good. All movies – whether fictional, semi-fictional, or documentary – need a "log line" and "pitch." They appear in all the ads. Does this log line and pitch interest you?

    The Log Line: At the height of World War II, two U.S. military intelligence officers meet near the Khyber Pass with a British agent. Their secret mission: To travel from Peshawar for 800 miles along the Indian-Afghan border, and thus to introduce America to the Great Game of Central Asia.

    Pitch: From *Lawrence of Arabia* to *Charlie Wilson's War*

If I have your attention now, let's take a minute to see what's in this book. It is intended to provide you with a good outline to make an interesting movie. The main elements are the same as in the plan for any movie.

The most important item in this book is the script for the movie. The other item is the script for the advertising piece, called the trailer script. Both the main script and the trailer script need a scenario, which is invisible to the public, but is important in marketing. In the case of *Three Men in a Jeep*, there are two scenarios – one for the main script, and one for the trailer. The two scenarios are registered with the Writers Guild of America-West. Each script has a specific copyright number, and each is registered with the U.S. copyright office.

The scripts in this book are typed the way movie scripts are supposed to be typed. The font is Courier 12, a larger typeface than is usual for a book; and the margins of the spoken parts of both the narrator (as voice over) and the actors (either on screen, or as v.o.) are much narrower than usual. This is to allow the narrator and actors to read the script from a distance, and to pace the movie at about one page per minute of screen time. In *Three Men*, there are fewer breaks than usual, and I read the 110-page script aloud in 132 minutes.

It is sometimes said that Hollywood is in a different world, and that Hollywood people speak a different language from the rest of us. But whether you like this or not, you need to obey Hollywood's rules, whether spoken or implied, to be successful in film-making.

You can find many books about how to write a Hollywood movie script, and how to sell it. These books give good examples of what to do, step by step, to write and sell a fictional or semi-fictional movie script. However, there is little or nothing in these books about how to write a successful script for a documentary movie. Nevertheless, I have been told that the basic rules still apply.

For example: A usual movie has a hero, who has flaws. He (or she) will eventually succeed in spite of the flaws. The hero will have an antagonist. One or more helpers will support the hero in his quest. Sherlock Holmes has his Dr. Watson as a helper; and Moriarty is the antagonist. In *Thee Men*, the hero is Gordon Enders, and his helper is Al Zimmermann, who, like Dr. Watson, records everything, and is usually non-judgmental. They are assisted by Sir Benjamin Bromhead, a strong but quiet man, like Sherlock's brother Mycroft. There may be a beautiful woman who supports the hero. In *Three Men*, it is Betty Crump Enders. She is the wife of Gordon Enders, who drives the jeep, "Ma Kabul." There are many anonymous antagonists who make trouble for the Three Men on the trip, but the principal one is the man known as the Faqir of Ipi. And there should be a great prize that they compete for, against all odds. It may be inanimate, such as the lost ark of Indiana Jones. In *Three Men*, it is the quest itself, to complete the journey of 800 miles. There should be three acts, each with a climax, not necessarily of the same length, and then a swift and dramatic end. The high point of the movie usually comes near the end of the second act. The third act may include a surprising twist. The movie flows seamlessly from one act to the next, in contrast to a play on a stage. The three acts in *Three Men* are outlined in the post-script notes. Movies often have flashbacks, and also signposts which point to future events. These tend to confuse the action, and should be used sparingly. *Three Men* utilizes a flashback at the start, but it then moves forward to the end.

If after reading this book, you find *Three Men in a Jeep* to be one that you might want to film, I suggest that you proceed step by step along this path:

1) Read the script aloud by yourself, keeping an eye on the clock. See how long it takes to read it through. You can change your voice, as if you were reading it to someone else. You could eventually do a trial film it that way, acting both as narrator and as the various actors, in voice overs.
2) Imagine what you could do with various scenes as you read them, using minimal backgrounds and props. A good way to start would be to use a quiet room with a white or matté wall for background, and a card table with a white cover sheet on which to place props.
3) If you want to film *Three Men*, a simple video camera would be a good way to start. For example, CyberlinkPowerDirector offers cameras and editing tools for less than $200.
4) The animation at the beginning of the movie can be simplified while you are making a trial film. Use a globe on a stand, and spin it by hand. Then use a large-scale map of Asia, covered with a clear plastic sheet; on this, use a broad Sharpie pen to outline the Himalaya Mountain Range in a red line, and large red dots, inserted one at a time, at the approximate locations of the great mountains: Mount Everest, K-2, and Nanda Devi. Then switch to a close-up map, focused on the Afghan-Pakistan border, centered on Peshawar, with Quetta at the edge of the map on the left and Chitral at an equal distance on the right. The route taken by the Three Men goes from Chitral to Quetta, and this can be traced with the red Sharpie. The mountain, Tirich Mir would be shown as a red dot just north of Chitral village. If your initial film is successful, you can substitute an animator's work for these three images at a later date. You should review the beginning of the film *Casablanca*, because it was my intent to model *Casablanca* for this imagery.
5) The images that appear during v.o.'s in the script can be scanned directly from my previous book, *"Dearest Barb" from Karachi*, using a closeup lens. However, if you later plan to make a film for distribution, you should recognize that these images are copyrighted by me (as shown on the copyright page), and permission to use them must be negotiated. If you wish to use copies of these images, which are in my personal files in jpg, you can contact me at the address shown below. I also have a copy on DVD of the movies taken by Zimmermann during World War II. This DVD is negotiable for you

to purchase and to use in making your film. I would follow usual Hollywood rules for guidance. If you are unable to locate me, the original photos and 16mm films are in Special Collections at the U.S. Naval Institute, Annapolis, Maryland.

6) Background music will enhance your film, and you may wish to pick some to use in your trial effort. Well-known tunes and songs from both World Wars and the period between the wars are readily available, but in most cases, you will need to obtain permission to use them in a film for distribution. For instance, consider "Lily Marlene," "Stardust," "The White Cliffs of Dover," and "As Time Goes By." Music from India and Central Asia can also be purchased, featuring a one- or two-stringed instrument.

7) If the initial film looks promising to you and your friends, and you would like to proceed, you must keep in mind the need to obtain the rights to make a movie. And you cannot make copies of the script without permission from the publisher, Heritage Books. You cannot make a movie for distribution without permission from both Heritage Books and the Naval Institute Press (the latter owns the movie rights to *Proceed to Peshawar*). The usual Hollywood rate for movie rights is 2.5 percent of the budget. To give some idea of costs, I have been told that the trailer could be filmed in three days for a cost of about $20,000; and a bare-bones budget for the full movie script would be about 30 days and $200,000. If the film were to be made on location in Asia, and if the actors were to use authentic period costumes and props, the cost would be much, much higher. You would also need a Hollywood lawyer to guide you through the necessary contracts, and then with his help, you would form an LLC. For a documentary such as *Three Men*, the trailer is the first step, because it can be used to find funding for a film based the full script.

None of these items present obstacles that cannot be overcome. They are typical steps in the making of Hollywood movies.

My address at present is:
George J. Hill
Khyber Pass Productions
3900 North Charles St., Room 901B
Baltimore, MD 21218-1716
(410) 366-1617
captgjh@yahoo.com
www.georgejhill.com

My lawyer's address is:
Michael E. Morales
Attorney at Law
10880 Wilshire Boulevard, Suite 2070
Los Angeles, CA 90024
Phone: (310) 278-0066
Fax: (310) 470-0044
michael@entatty.com

_____

Some useful references on film-making are:
• Kenneth Atchity, *Sell Your Story to Hollywood: Writer's Pocket Guide to the Business of Show Business* (Los Angeles: Story Merchant Books, 2016)
• Jonathan Sanger, *Making the Elephant Man: A Producer's Memoir* (Jefferson, NC: MacFarland & Co., 2016)
• Blake Snyder, *Save the Cat: The Last Book on Screenwriting You'll Ever Need* (Studio City, CA: Michael Wiese Productions, 2005)

Prologue
A Movie Plan Begins and Evolves

In February 2016, I was hard at work on a documentary movie based on my book, *Proceed to Peshawar*. Nine months earlier, this book (published by the U.S. Naval Institute) had won a Finalist's Medal at the Indie Book Award Festival. I had decided to work on a movie about this book instead of giving more lectures about it. But on 2 February 2016, I received a cold call from a Hollywood producer/agent named **Harvey Rochman.** He said, "I believe your book could be a good movie. Let's work on this together." Harvey soon came up with the title, *Khyber Pass*, and the idea of making a semi-fictional movie instead of a true story or biopic. *Khyber Pass* would be a spy story, based on the adventuresome and somewhat mysterious driver of the jeep in *Proceed to Peshawar*, Major Gordon Enders. Harvey said that his friends **Ed Asner**, **Kevin Conner**, and **Howard Kazanjian** would soon be in touch with me. I of course recognized the name of Ed Asner, but I had only a vague notion of who Kevin and Howard were. An internet search soon showed me that they had done important work in directing and producing movies.

    A man who said he was Ed Asner called me at dinner a few days after Harvey's first call. I had serious doubts that he was really the famous actor. However, he assured me that he was, indeed, the man who I remembered so well, "Lou Grant," from *The Mary Tyler Moore Show*. As we ended the conversation, he said, "George, don't let those Hollywood bastards get you down." Good advice. The internet showed me that Ed was a seven-time Primetime Emmy Awards winner, and that he had been president of the Screen Actors Guild in 1981-1985. Kevin Connor soon called, and he left an email message: "I shall try and call tomorrow from the set and look forward to hearing about this wonderful project that Harvey has briefly told me about." I looked up Kevin on the internet and saw that he was a film and TV director with credits for more than 100 films, including *The Return of Sherlock Holmes; Frankenstein, and Great Expectations.* He would offer much help with *Khyber Pass* over the next two years. Howard Kazanjian soon sent an e-mail, saying "Khyber Pass is a wonderful project and I do hope it gets made." A quick glance at Wikipedia showed that Howard was formerly vice president of production of Lucasfilms, and that he had produced *Return of the Jedi* and was executive producer of *Raiders of the Lost Ark.* Harvey arranged for me to have dinner in March 2016 with Ed Asner and others, including two prospective script writers, **John Hertzler** and **Toni Nagy.** John made several very useful suggestions, but he decided to bow out of the project. Toni agreed to write a script after she finished her current project. Ed won my heart at that time by writing on the title page of *Proceed to Peshawar*, "This is a big treat. I'm honored." After the first script was completed by Toni Nagy, Howard Kazanjian offered a long critique, concluding with encouraging comments. Howard suggested that the project needed a big goal, similar to the ark in the film that he produced, *Raiders of the Lost Ark.* He warned that it is also "a high budgeted picture." I eventually learned that the budget for a film like this would be somewhere between $10M and $200M!!

    Over the next few months, I learned a lot about Hollywood's rules for making movies. **Rick Russell**, Director of the U.S. Naval Institute, introduced me to the USNI's agent, **Steven Moore** of the Kohner Agency. Steven advised me to get a Hollywood lawyer. He suggested **Michael Morales**, whose office was near his on Wiltshire Boulevard. Michael led me through the process of forming an LLC and he drafted all the other legal documents that I have needed: to hire script writers, to form an LLC, to obtain the option for rights to make a film, and to secure copyright on the script(s). I learned from him about unfamiliar terms such as CoA (Certificate of Agreement) and NDA (Non-Disclosure Agreement). Morales thought that **Les Klinger**, also on Wiltshire Boulevard, could be my LLC lawyer. I learned to use the websites for IMDb (Internet Movie Database), Rotten Tomatoes, Wikipedia, and Google to do research on people who were introduced to me by Harvey. Through Harvey, I met with **Ken Atchity** and got good advice from him, and also **Norm Stephens**. Ken has many Hollywood credits and he wrote an encouraging inscription for me in his book, *Sell Your Story to Hollywood.* Norm is an Emmy and Peabody Award-winning producer, who recalled growing up in New Jersey. **Tim Zimmermann**, who co-wrote and was associate producer of the documentary *Blackfish*, is my wife's nephew. He said that Hollywood "is awash with money, but you need an agent to tap into it." I learned that a good Hollywood agent will only accept you and your project if it looks very promising, but not for hire – rather, for a share in the income. I never was able to find an agent who would accept the *Khyber Pass* project on those terms.

Toni Nagy completed a first draft of her script in December 2016. By coincidence, I planned to be in southern California for a family vacation in the first week of January 2017. Harvey suggested that I host a "meet and greet" in Santa Monica to introduce the plan for *Khyber Pass* to his friends. With Harvey's help, we held a party for twenty-two at the famous Shutters on the Beach for the unveiling of Toni's script. It was a wonderful evening. **Jonathan Sanger**, who produced *The Elephant Man*, was there; he wrote a nice inscription on the title page of *Proceed to Peshawar*, thanking Harvey for introducing us. **Jim Steele**, a film producer and senior consultant at Global Cinema Initiatives, wrote "Congrats on the book," and that he hoped that the rest of my life would be as interesting as this. Serious discussions followed over the next several weeks with producers, actors, and movie financiers. **Galen Walker,** director of the latest two *Ninja Turtles* movies, and **Ian Merrick**, producer and director of *Black Panther*, each offered to work on the project, if I could reach a satisfactory arrangement with either of them. Sad to say, we couldn't come to terms. And as usually is the case in Hollywood, I was advised that a second script writer would need to become involved. Harvey suggested that I hire **Joe Verrastro**, who had been working successfully with Ed on some of his recent "shoots." Ed Asner supported this proposal, so I met with Joe at my home in New Jersey in the summer of 2017. He completed his re-write in September 2017. Joe also wrote a short script for a prologue, in which Ed Asner would play the role of my father-in-law, remembering the trip he took in 1943 with the other two men. Ed gave a verbal ok to do this. However, I couldn't locate anyone else who would invest in the film. I had by then spent $70,000 and two years of hard work on it. I didn't want to be the sole investor in this project. So in February 2018, I finally said quits to *Khyber Pass* and returned to my plan to write a documentary movie, *Three Men in a Jeep*.

I took my script for *Three Men* to JHU-MICA (Johns Hopkins University-Maryland Institute College of Art), and it was circulated to the staff. I talked with one of the faculty members about it. I was told that it was too big a project for anyone there to take on at this time. However, one of the staff members suggested that I might apply for a grant to make the documentary film, using a trailer. My trailer script also got good reviews from those who read it. However, I decided that instead, I would make the two scripts available for sale, and that I would try to help anyone who wanted to use it.

Other Comments on the Film Project as It Developed

"You have a good story to tell and the advantage of a good head on your shoulders."
-- A writer / producer / publicist (24 August 2016)

"I have analyzed your proposed script for the trailer . . . We will need to find a narrator . . . We also have Gordon Enders speaking at the end. . . . The bulk of the visuals are motion graphics."
-- A film director / producer / editor (21 June 2018)

"Wow! I like it George! Very clever. And yes, documentaries also have log lines and pitch."
-- A film director and producer (23 June 2018)

MOVIE MAKING
Partial list of those who have read the script (*) and/or offered to assist
• Present at "Meet and Greet" at Shutters on the Beach, Santa Monica, 28 December 2016
Many listed below have credits in several fields. For example, a producer may also be a director and writer.

Khyber Pass

Instigator
*Harvey Rochman

Publisher
Richard Russell – Naval Institute Press

Agents
Steven Moore – Kohner Agency
*Terry Rindall
Humaira Ghilzai
Pamela Lynne
Weston Middleton, for Bradley Cooper

Lawyers
Michael Morales, Esq.
Leslie Klinger, Esq.

Producers
* Howard Kazanjian
• Jonathan Sanger
* • Galen Walker – MediaToaster
* • Ian Merrick – Epiphany Films, Inc.
* Ken Atchity – Atchity Productions, LLC
* Norman Stephens
Tim Zimmermann

Directors
* Kevin Connor
* Michael Mercier
* • Randall Kleiser
Luis Mandoki
* Rolando Vinas

Marketing
* Kevin Winston - DigitLA

Actors
* • Ed Asner
• Pius Savage
Jeff McCarthy

Writers
John Hertzler
* Toni Nagy
* Joe Verrastro
* Roger Williams

Financiers
• Joseph (J. J.) Barmettler
• Jim Steele
Porter Bibb
* Gaurav Bhalla
* Patrick J. Creamer – Revelation Studios

Others
* • Frank Kwong, M.D.
* Betty Kwong
Patty Hoenigman
Maynard Creel
Gertrude Enders Huntington, Ph.D.
* Chelsea Milojkovic – webmistress
Gregory Nagy, Ph.D
Robert Naud
* Ambassador James Jeffrey

Three Men in a Jeep
* Will Bryson – JHU-MICA (Johns Hopkins University-Maryland Institute College of Art)
* Robert Cole, Elite Video Solutions
* Rod Lopez, New Style Independent Pictures
* Masud Roshan – CEO, Technical Resources Group

Masud Roshan was born in Kabul, Afghanistan. His family left Afghanistan and relocated to Pakistan when he was young. He grew up in Peshawar, near the Khyber Pass, and spent his childhood years there. The family came to America and he attended the University of Maryland, and his sisters have Harvard degrees. He identifies as Pashtun. He says that my book, *Proceed to Peshawar*, is authentic, and that the two American officers must have learned the customs of the Pashtuns - *Pashtunwali*.

THE MOVIE

Three Men in a Jeep Called "Ma Kabul"

Log Line & Pitch

The Log Line: At the height of World War II, two U.S. military intelligence officers meet near the Khyber Pass with a British agent. Their Secret mission: To travel from Peshawar for 800 miles along the border of India and Afghanistan, to introduce America to the Great Game of Central Asia.

Pitch: From *Lawrence of Arabia* to *Charlie Wilson's War*

Introduction

I have heard it said by many in Hollywood that "It often takes ten years to make a movie." Well, this movie has been moving slower than that – it's been 75 years, and still counting.

My father-in-law, Albert Zimmermann, was a camera buff. He started making 16mm home movies when he married Barbara Shoemaker in Philadelphia in 1926. He left more than fifty 8-inch reels of film in his home when he died. He carefully edited and spliced them together. Two additional reels were taken when he was on duty as a Naval Intelligence Officer in India in World War II. They were filed separately at his home, along with a scrapbook that contained his wartime papers, and other items – including more than 300 photographs and nearly 200 letters that he wrote to his wife. I am sure that he intended to do something more with the movies that he took on the trip in 1943 along the North-West Frontier border with Afghanistan, but he never got a chance to do it. He died suddenly in 1961, at age 59. The films that he took in World War II were separated from his other home movies. After Zimmermann died, Barbara kept them in their house until she died in 1985. And then the movie films, photos, scrapbook, letters, and his other wartime papers passed to his daughter Barbara, known as "Babs." The films, photos, notes and other documents lay undisturbed in Bab's attic. They rested there until 2007, when Babs was getting ready to move to a retirement home. She offered them to her sister Helene – who is my wife.

Over the next five years, I spent part of my time studying Zimmermann's wartime papers. My research took me to the National Archives and to several other academic archives. I accumulated a library of more 100 books as I gradually understood what Al Zimmermann was doing in India from 1943 until 1945. The most interesting part of his work was a one-month trip that he took with two other intelligence officers along the border of Afghanistan in November-December 1943. The trip, which I call "Three Men in a Jeep," was taken in the open; the two Americans – Navy Lieutenant Zimmermann and Army Major Gordon Enders – were in uniform. They were greeted by hereditary princes, high-ranking British officers, and tribal leaders. But they also had secret orders: to study how Britain maintained peace along the Border, in order to prepare for a transition to American involvement in this area in the post-war period. They had to learn about *Pashtunwali* – the customs of the tribal people – because this was the key to keeping peace on the Border. And they were on the lookout for Russian penetration, as had always been a concern in the time of the Raj, when the India was the "Jewel in the Crown" of the British Empire. The long struggle between Britain and Russia for control of India was known as the Great Game, after Kipling' use of this term in his novel *Kim* in 1900.

The British departed from India sooner than most thought possible – it was in 1947 when Independence and Partition took place. However, America's interest in this area – the Border of Afghanistan and Pakistan – remained dormant for another thirty years, because other areas in the world – Europe, Korea, Vietnam, Cuba – took precedence in the Cold War with the Soviet Union. But the American public suddenly saw Afghanistan in a new light when the Soviet Union invaded it in 1979, and this area has never since fully receded from view. The Soviet Union withdrew from Afghanistan in 1989, and the USSR collapsed. There was then a reorganization in Central Asia, as Russia and five former Soviet Republics developed an independent relationship that was no longer under control by Moscow. And Afghanistan came under control of a fundamentalist Islamic organization known as the Taliban. The attacks by al Qaeda on America on 11 September 2001 were organized by Osama bin Laden, who had found a safe haven and shelter by the Taliban in Afghanistan. The Taliban operated along both sides of the Afghan-Pakistan Border. This is the Border that was first traversed by Americans in the trip by Lt. Zimmermann and Maj. Gordon Enders in November-December 1943.

When Lieutenant Zimmermann flew to India in June 1943, he passed through Casablanca on his way to Cairo, and then to Karachi. It was only a little more than seven months after the beginning of Operation TORCH – the Allied invasion of North Africa – and it was less than two months after the last Axis forces surrendered there. The invasion soon freed Casablanca from control by the Vichy French government and the Nazi forces, which included the German Afrika Corps under Field Marshal Rommel, and Italian Army troops. The movie *Casablanca* had been filmed California in 1942, just before the landing force arrived in North Africa. *Casablanca* was released in January 1943, and it received great publicity because of the invasion. It is one of the most famous movies ever made. In the Script for "Three Men," you will see that I have intentionally re-used the opening scene of the movie *Casablanca*, which shows a spinning globe, dissolving to a map of the area of interest. I think Zimmermann would appreciate this, and so, too, would his senior officer, Commander (later Captain) Gene Markey. Zimmermann and Markey first met in Cairo on their way to India. Before the war, Markey was a very successful Hollywood movie producer, as well as being an undercover Navy Reserve Intelligence officer. He was also a man about town, who had been married to two famous actresses – first to Joan Bennett, and then to Hedy Lamarr. He was a close friend of the director, John Ford, also a Navy Reserve officer. (Both men became Rear Admirals after the war.) Six years earlier, Markey had produced the movie *Wee Willie Winkie*, starring Shirley Temple, in her favorite role. The movie was directed by Ford. It was based on a story by Rudyard Kipling. The movie was set in the Border area of Afghanistan and India – the same area that was traversed by Three Men in a Jeep, although it was actually shot in California. It is tantalizing to consider whether Markey and Zimmermann could have discussed Markey's career in the movie business, given Zimmermann's interest and skills as an amateur movie-maker. Markey had already been decorated for undercover action while he was on the staff of Admiral William "Bull" Halsey in the Pacific, and he became a close friend of Admiral Lord Louis Mountbatten in Ceylon. After the war, Markey married a third time, to the actress Myrna Loy, with Halsey as his best man. In 1965, Ford directed the movie *In Harm's Way*, starring John Wayne and Henry Fonda, in which "Commander Egan Powell," played by Burgess Meredith, is based on Markey.

When I finished my research on my father-in-law's wartime papers and the connections of these papers to other events, I wrote a manuscript for a book which I called *Proceed to Peshawar*. I finished the manuscript in 2012, and submitted it to four academic presses. It was rejected by all four. I then sent it to the Naval Institute Press, which accepted it, but said it was too long; I would have to eliminate much of the background information, and also many of the photos that Lieutenant Zimmermann took on the Trip. I saved the original manuscript, and it has been useful in preparing the script for the movie, *Three Men in a Jeep*. The Naval Institute Press' version was published in 2013, and it won a Finalist's Medal at the Indie Book Awards festival in December 2015.

I planned to make a documentary film based on the book. It would incorporate voice overs from an invisible Narrator and it would utilize actors who would play the roles of several men and women who are no longer alive. Their words would be taken from published documents. But in February 2016, just as I was about to start on this project, I received a phone call, a "cold call," from a man who said his name was Harvey Rochman – a Hollywood producer or agent, who now lived in Key West, Florida. Harvey said that although he hadn't yet read the book, he believed that *Proceed to Peshawar* would be a great basis for a movie – a semi-fictional movie, as he called it. He thought that Gordon Enders would be the principal character, and that his career could be featured in a series of films. Harvey suggested the title *Khyber Pass* for the first movie in this series. We found that title *Khyber Pass* had never been used in a film shot in America, and it appeared to be a good start on what would be a major project. Within a day or two after Harvey's first call to me, he called again to say that Ed Asner would be calling me, and that his friends Kevin Connor and Howard Kazanjian would be advising us on the project. Sure enough, Ed Asner did call, and then Kevin Connor. Ed and I had many conversations over the years from February 2016 until February 2018. We had dinner near Baltimore with a screen writer and my family, and again in Santa Monica with him and his family. Harvey introduced me to many people in the Hollywood film industry, and I enjoyed every one of their calls and meetings over the following two years. We tried very hard to make a *Khyber Pass* movie. I purchased the sole option on the screen rights to *Proceed to Peshawar* from the Naval Institute Press; I got a Hollywood lawyer; I set up Khyber Pass Productions, LLC; I hired a script writer and registered her script with the Writers Guild of America, and got a copyright on it; together, we set up a website (Khyber Pass Movie) to market the production; and then I hired another script writer and registered his script in the same way; he wrote another short script for a Prologue. But Harvey and I couldn't find anyone else to invest anything in to the project. And, sadly, after two years, I decided to call an end to the *Khyber Pass* movie project. I wound it down and dissolved the LLC. And I returned to the previous plan to do a documentary film.

One of the most important things I learned from what I call my "Hollywood caper" is how the movie business actually works. We had a "meet and greet" at Shutters-on-the-Beach in January 2017 with twenty-two people, including seven friends of Harvey who were well-known as actors/financiers/producers/directors/writers (one or more categories). And on the same trip, my family and I visited the Paramount Studios as tourists. We got a lot of advice that has been both interesting and useful. Perhaps most importantly, I learned what a movie script should look like. And that a movie needs a "tag line" and "pitch." And so forth. One of my new friends, a busy screen writer, kindly sent me a copy of the script for *Casablanca*. He told me – and it is also on the script he sent – that the actual script for *Casablanca* is not available, because it was written and changed each day, as the movie was being filmed. Nevertheless, I have followed that outline in writing the script for this documentary movie.

As I returned to work on the documentary movie in February 2018, I studied the files of the Zimmermann Wartime Papers that were in my computer. I found much material there that had not previously been published, including the letters that Zimmermann wrote to his wife from Karachi and more than 150 previously unpublished photographs. I assembled this material into a large book, which I called *"Dearest Barb" from Karachi, 1943-1945*. Heritage Books accepted it for publication in 2018. The documentary film *Three Men in a Jeep Called*

"Ma Kabul" is based on the historic trip along the southern border of Afghanistan, with a secret mission, that was taken in the fall of 1943 by U.S. Navy Lieutenant Albert Zimmermann, U.S. Army Major Gordon Bandy Enders, and British Major Sir Benjamin Bromhead.

I am now 85 years old. I have written and copyrighted a Script for the documentary movie, which I call "Three Men in a Jeep" and I have registered its Scenario with the Writers Guild of America-West. I have also written a Script for a Trailer, and I copyrighted and registered it. I am ready now to pause. It is time for others to study these Scripts and Scenarios to see what they may do with them. I would like to help with this, if I am able to do so.

THREE MEN IN A JEEP

SCENARIO

This is a true story. It tells the story of a trip taken in Central Asia by three military intelligence officers at the height of World War II. In November 1943, the three men – two Americans and one British – traveled along the southern border of Afghanistan to reach the village of Chitral. It was the most remote place in British India. The palace of the hereditary ruler, the Mehtar of Chitral, was only 24 miles from the unclimbed summit of Tirich Mir. It was the highest mountain in the Hindu Kush range – the westernmost mountains of the Himalayas. In their jeep, in spite of warnings of snow and ice ahead, they crossed the Lowari Pass into Chitral. No motor vehicle had ever before tried to cross that pass. Along the way, they exchanged tributes with two other hereditary rulers, the Wali of Swat and the Nawab of Dir. The British officer, Major Sir Benjamin Bromhead, and the Mehtar of Chitral were both new in their positions. They needed to meet each other and exchange the gifts that were customary. Because of its geographic location in Central Asia, Chitral had long been contested between the British, the Russians, and the Afghans. Britain, having won Chitral by force of arms in the late 19th century, was determined to keep it within its Empire. Two Americans, Army Major Gordon Enders and Navy Lieutenant Albert Zimmermann, were assigned to go on a trip with Bromhead along most of the Afghan-Indian Border, from Chitral in the north to Quetta in the south. Their trip, in Enders' jeep, began in the ancient city of Peshawar in India – now Pakistan – which for many centuries had been the gateway to the Khyber Pass into Afghanistan. After the travelers returned from Chitral to Peshawar, they traveled south through the mountainous, dangerous, tribal territory of Waziristan to reach the city of Quetta, in Baluchistan. The journey that the Americans took along the Afghan Border – the Durand Line – was over 800 miles as the crow flies, but much longer in their jeep. No Americans had ever before attempted to take this trip, and none would ever do it again. The American officers were in uniform, armed, and under official orders.

As the film begins, we see an animated globe, spinning to a stop. It fades to a map showing the Afghan-Indian Border, in the westernmost part of the Himalayas. The image of Tirich Mir mountain appears, and then across the face of it, the words: "November 1943." A Narrator, with V.O., ties together the many scenes that follow, interspersed with actors who speak the lines of different characters, using words from their letters, books, reports, and other documents from archives. The Narrator tells that in November 1943, President Franklin Roosevelt, Prime Minister Winston Churchill, and Generalissimo Chiang Kai-shek were meeting at the Cairo Conference, code named SEXTANT, to plan for the next moves in the war, and to begin planning for the post-war world. This moment in time was what Churchill referred to in 1950 as "The Hinge of Fate." We hear a brief conversation between the three intelligence officers, in which they agree to disregard the warnings of danger and proceed with their attempt to cross the Lowari Pass. The movie then has a flashback to the early lives of each of the three men, continuing to the beginning of World War I in 1914.

Gordon Enders is shown to be the son of a Presbyterian missionary who came from Iowa to India. Enders grew up on the Indian-Tibetan border, with a Tibetan guru as his mentor. He believed that he would follow the career of the boy-spy, *Kim*, based on Kipling's novel of the same name, which was published at about the time he was in India. Bromhead was a titled Englishman, fifth in a line of the Baronets of Thurlby Hall in Lincolnshire. He was a professional military officer, who had been wounded and decorated with the Order of the British Empire. Zimmermann was a wealthy socialite from Philadelphia. He was the son of an immigrant from Germany who became a successful inventor and businessman. Zimmermann had quietly been recruited into intelligence work before the war, and he was sent to Karachi in July 1943. Neither Bromhead or Zimmermann were involved with World War I.

The flashbacks shift to a montage of scenes of battles on land, on sea, and in the air in World War I. The names of many characters who will later appear in the movie are seen overlying the battle scenes. The last name shown is Gordon Enders. As a pilot in the U.S. Army, he falls from a plane in France, over Savenay, Brittany, without a parachute. He is thought initially to be dead. But he survived the fall, and was nursed back to health by Betty Crump, who he marries in 1919. Gordon Enders becomes the central figure in this movie. His career as an undercover intelligence officer for the U.S. government is shown probably to have started in 1920, when he is sent out to China as a junior officer in the Department of Commerce, and it continues until he retires from the Army as a colonel in 1962.

The period between World War I and World War II (1920-1939) is shown in a series of apparently unrelated scenes of events in China, England, and America. Gordon Enders becomes a businessman who sells Corsair bombers to Chiang Kai-shek, and he becomes Chiang's private pilot. He is introduced to the ruler of Tibet, the 9th Panchan Lama, by the Generalissimo and Mdme. Chiang, and he flies gold dust for the Panchan from Tibet to Shanghai. His work in China comes to a sudden end in 1937, when the Panchan dies and the Japanese invasion of China reaches Shanghai. Then, a scene showing a dinner party in London in 1936 introduces Rex Benson, a wealthy banker and secret intelligence officer, who will later become the British military attaché in Washington. In the fall of 1941, Benson provides a card of introduction for Enders, the newly appointed U.S. military attaché to Afghanistan, which Enders presents to the Governor of the North-West Frontier Province in Peshawar, India. Enders believes that with this introduction, he can achieve the goal of his dreams: Like the fictional boy-spy Kim, Enders hopes to travel along the Border, looking for Russian spies. Zimmerman believes that Enders "instigated" the Trip. We learn that it was probably more complicated than that. Many people were interested in having Americans make this Trip, and Enders and Zimmermann were selected because they were the best men to do it. Britain wanted to show the U.S. what its problems are along the Border – with the Pathan tribesmen and their rulers – and how they had learned to deal with these problems. Why? Because many Englishmen believe that after World War II is over, India will become independent, and the U.S. will take over Britain's role in the Great Game. And for many years, FDR has quietly been thinking along the same lines. We learn that even before he became president, he had wanted to find a role for the U.S. in Tibet. In 1942, FDR dispatched an O.S.S. team to Tibet to make friends with the new Dalai Lama. The O.S.S. team was grudgingly given permission to go to Lhasa by the British in India. They believed that FDR was encroaching on their territory. And then, the O.S.S. team was withdrawn early in 1943, at the insistence of China. Tibet was then out of FDR's reach, but FDR would know that Enders' plan to take a trip along the Border would put the U.S. back into the Great Game. And it did.

The main portion of the movie consists of many images, and comments by Zimmermann and Bromhead, as the Three Men travel along the Border of the North-West Frontier Province in 1943 – scenes of danger, beauty, and intrigue. After the Three Men return to Peshawar and complete the first part of their Trip, Enders disappears for more than three days. The movie speculates that he may have flown to Cairo, to brief FDR and Chiang on what he has seen. The Viceroy, Field Marshal Archibald Wavell, comes to Peshawar at that time, and he hears about the Trip from Gordon Enders. Zimmermann wrote to his wife, saying sarcastically that Enders "loves to talk, and modesty isn't one of his virtues." The Three Men proceed in a heavily armed convoy through the dangerous mountain tribal territory of North and South Waziristan. They pass tank traps that were set to prevent Rommel from getting to India, they dodge rifle fire from brigands and rebel tribesmen, and they listen to return fire from British machine guns. They watch shelling from British guns, and bombs being dropped by the R.A.F. Zimmermann comments, sardonically, that the bombs "had good moral effect." After many adventures, and additional trips to the Afghan Border, the Three Men finally reach Quetta safely, and they go their separate ways: Enders to Kabul, Bromhead to Peshawar, and Zimmermann to Karachi.

In the final part of the movie, we learn what happens to the Three Men. Enders returns twice to Kabul, in January and February 1944. On his first return, he briefs Major General Patrick Hurley on the situation in Afghanistan, and he returns again with Major Ernest Fox, who replaces him as military attaché. Enders is invalided home with malaria in March 1944, and he is then sent to the Pacific for the rest of the war. His later career in military intelligence and in civilian life after he retires is briefly told. Betty Enders died in 1962 and he died in 1978. Bromhead's later life is described in India until it becomes independent in 1947, and in England thereafter. And Zimmermann enjoys returning to civilian life, but he died suddenly in 1961.

Three Acts

There is no break in the Script, but there is a natural division in it, which divides it into three acts, as follows:

Act I - Prelude, with backgrounds of each of the Three Men, and a climax when they meet in Peshawar, India, in November 1943, to start their trip along the border of Afghanistan.

Act II, Part I - The Three Men ascend to the most remote place in India -- Chitral -- after crossing the Lowari Pass in a jeep. Their passage over the Lowari is the first-ever made in a motor vehicle. The climax of this part is when they return to Peshawar to meet and are debriefed by the Viceroy of India, Field Marshal Archibald Wavell. He had crossed the pass as a young officer on horseback, and he remembered how difficult it was.

Act II, Part II - The Three Men continue through very dangerous and hostile Tribal Territory (Waziristan) to Quetta, Baluchistan. The climax is when they finally reach Quetta safely and are debriefed and go on a picnic with the Governor and his family.

Act III - Aftermath, in which the Three Men go their separate ways, and the war ends. One of them, Gordon Enders, returns twice to Afghanistan and he then returns to the U.S. with malaria. The return trips of Enders to Kabul are dramatic, but in Act III, there is a gradual denouement, without a climax.

THREE MEN IN A JEEP

By George Hill

A Documentary Film,
set in Central Asia in World War II

FADE IN:

INSERT - A black screen, on which a small bright dot appears. It slowly enlarges to be seen as a revolving globe. The globe stops spinning and it is enlarged to focus on a map of Asia.

> NARRATOR (V.O.)
> Across Asia - from East to West -
> there are many ranges of mountains
> - known collectively as the
> Himalayas.

The map fades to a diagram, showing the borders of China, India, Pakistan, Afghanistan, and the former Soviet republics, including Russia, Uzbekistan, and Tajikistan, as they are in 2018. The Himalayas are red-lined.

> Some of the highest mountains in
> the world are in the Himalayas -
> Mount Everest, K-2, and Nanda Devi.

Red dots appear on the map to show each of these mountains, and the map changes to show the names and borders of countries in 1943.

> Further west is the range known as
> the Hindu Kush, where the borders
> of four countries meet at the
> Wakhan Peninsula of Afghanistan. In
> 1943, only the narrow strip of the
> Wakhan separated the Soviet Union
> from India.

The borders of Chitral appear on the map, and a red dot for Tirich Mir mountain. Red-line the Hindu Kush range.

FADE IN: Image of Tirich Mir.

> The highest mountain in the Hindu Kush is Tirich Mir. Its south face towers over a small village, in a kingdom ruled for many centuries by the Mehtar of Chitral. It was the most remote place in British India in 1943.

"November 1943" appears on the image of Tirich Mir mountain.

> At the height of World War II, as the Allies were slowly advancing against their enemies in Europe and the Pacific, President Franklin Roosevelt and Prime Minister Winston Churchill planned to meet in Cairo, Egypt, with Chiang Kai-shek to discuss their next moves, and the future of the post-war world. In 1950, Churchill referred to this crucial moment as "The Hinge of Fate."

The title words for the film, "Three Men in a Jeep" appear below "November 1943" on the image of Tirich Mir.

> And at the same time, three Allied military officers - two Americans and one an Englishman - were ordered to proceed to Chitral in an American jeep. Who were they? Why

> were they sent there? And what did
> they find?

DISSOLVE TO:

Image of Malakand, North-West Frontier Province, at the British Political Agent's residence. THREE MEN converse.

> MAJOR SIR BENJAMIN BROMHEAD
> I've just received a telegram from our political officer in Chitral. He says, "Ice, snow, and mud on Lowari Pass. Advise against any attempt to cross it." Gordon, What say you?

> MAJOR GORDON ENDERS, U.S. ARMY
> We'll make it, Benjie. Zimmermann?

> LT AL ZIMMERMANN, U.S.N.R.
> I'm game for it, too. Let's go.

CUT TO:

Image of three men in a jeep, on the summit of Lowari Pass, from the cover of *Proceed to Peshawar*.

DISSOLVE TO:

Image of Thurlyby Hall, England. Montage of Battles of Saratoga and Waterloo and Rourke's Drift; of India, Wellington College, and a Baronet's medal.

> NARRATOR (V.O.)
> In 1943, as a hereditary Baronet, Sir Benjamin Bromhead, age 43, ranked highest in the social order of the British Raj in the North-West Frontier Province of India. India was then the "Jewel of the British Empire." Sir Benjie

believed, as did many in the province, that India would become free after the war. They thought that India would be partitioned, and that the North-West Frontier Province would become part of a new nation, Pakistan.

[pause]

Major Sir Benjamin was the 5th Baronet Bromhead of Thurlby Hall, Lincolnshire, England. His ancestors had been in military service in India for three generations. Long before, they had been prominent in England. The first baronet was wounded and captured at Saratoga in America in 1777, and the third baronet fought at the battle of Waterloo. Benjie's great-uncle, Lieutenant Gonville Bromhead, won the Victoria Cross at the Battle of Rourke's Drift in Africa, and was buried in Allahabad, India. Michael Caine played Gonville Bromhead in the movie *Zulu*. Benjie's father died when he was 10, and he thus became the successor to the baronetcy when his grandfather, the 4th baronet, died. Benjie was sent to England to be educated, and in 1914 he was a student at England's premier boarding school – Wellington College – when World War I broke out.

CUT TO:

MONTAGE – Images of John and Eva (Kellenbenz) Zimmermann, their home and his factories in Philadelphia, the Zimmermann family, and images of their children.

NARRATOR (V.O.)

Albert Zimmermann was the youngest of the three officers on this trip. At age 41, he was the most successful son of a poor immigrant who had achieved the American Dream. His father came to America as a young man, having been trained as a weaver by his father in Germany. In Philadelphia, Al's father invented new techniques of weaving and dyeing, and he became a partner in Artloom, one of the largest carpet manufacturers in America. Al grew up near his father's factory in a grand house with servants. He attended public schools and the University of Pennsylvania, where he was president of the Glee Club. He was a member of Sphinx, a secret society. In 1917, after America entered World War I, one of Al's brothers was a soldier in the American Army in Europe. The father of Barbara Shoemaker, who Al later married, was also in Europe as the Chief of Ophthalmology for the American Expeditionary Forces. At age 15, Al knew about World War I, but he was not personally involved in it.

CUT TO:

MONTAGE - Images of the Enders family in Iowa, of Gordon Enders as a boy, and file photos of rural Iowa in 1897, a passenger train in Chicago in about 1903, a passenger ship on the Atlantic at about that time, and docks in Philadelphia, Liverpool, and Calcutta, India, in 1903.

                    NARRATOR (V.O.)

> Gordon Enders was the oldest of the three Allied officers who were poised to cross the Lowari pass into Chitral in November 1943. He called himself "an American Kim," for the boy-spy who was the hero in Kipling's novel, *Kim*. He had long dreamed of making this trip, and he is said to have instigated it. He had acquired all of the skills necessary to do it. In October 1941, he was sent to Kabul, Afghanistan, as the U.S. Military Attaché. In December 1941, shortly before Pearl Harbor was attacked, he crossed the Khyber Pass into Afghanistan. He was the first American diplomat to be stationed in Afghanistan. He came back across the Khyber Pass to meet the other two officers in Peshawar, India, at the start of this trip. [pause] Gordon Enders was born in rural Iowa in 1897. His father was a Presbyterian minister, and his mother was a teacher. Reverend Enders and his wife decided to go to India as missionaries in 1903.

MONTAGE - Images of the Enders family in India: group picture of the family, and file photos of India in about 1903-1910, the mountain, Nanda Devi, and of Tibet, from Enders' book, *Nowhere Else in the World*.

NARRATOR (V.O.)
The three Enders children - Miriam,
Gordon, and Bob - would spend much
of their childhood in rural India.
The family first lived at Etawah
near the Grand Trunk Road. They
then moved to Almorah, near the
foot of the great sacred mountain,
Nanda Devi.

Image of cover of the book, and then of Enders, from his book. In 1935, in his book, *Nowhere Else in the World* Gordon recalled his childhood in India:

GORDON ENDERS
Almorah was one tiny unit in
India's northern frontier line of
defense, which stretched from
Afghanistan to Burma. The
situation to the north of Almorah
was dangerous, where the forbidden
and secretive land of Tibet was the
focus of an imperialistic drama in
which England, China and Russia
were the principal actors. The
first language I learned in India
was the Hindustani of the plains,
to which I soon added the Tibetan
polyglot patois spoken in Almorah.
Jowar Singh, a Hindu hillman, was
our devoted mentor and teacher.
But a far more important figure in
turning my life toward its eventual
goal was Jowar's father-in-law, a
remarkable Tibetan named Chanti. I
had read Kipling's *Kim*, and I
recognized that Chanti's work was
somehow a part of the British
Intelligence Service. Some of his
visitors were "Kim-men." The first

>   Chinese I ever met was the trader,
>   Wu Ming-fu, from Chengdu. Masih
>   Ulla, was my Mohammaden friend, and
>   from him I learned about the
>   customs of the Muslims.

MONTAGE - images from the early 20th century of Wooster, Ohio, and the College of Wooster, Chautauqua, Col. William Eddy, early biplanes, Norton-Harjes Ambulance Unit, World War I ambulances, and French Foreign Legion airplanes of World War I.

>   GORDON ENDERS
>   I was sent back to America in 1910
>   to finish high school and prepare
>   for college in Wooster, Ohio. I
>   was there for five years.
>   Children of other missionaries were
>   with me in the dormitory. Nowhere
>   else in America could such a
>   strangely assorted group be found.
>   Not a single one of the fifty had
>   less than two languages; some spoke
>   a half-dozen strange tongues. Our
>   evenings were filled with tales of
>   travel and adventure. Bill Eddy
>   spoke almost casually of mass
>   deportation, starvation and
>   slaughter of the Armenians in Asia
>   Minor. I had finished my freshman
>   year when the World War broke out
>   in Europe. The declarations of war
>   came during the summer vacation,
>   when I was working at the
>   Chautauqua Assembly grounds.
>   During the early part of that
>   August, I saw my first airplane
>   flights, which stirred me more than
>   anything I can remember, and I was
>   on the lookout for a way to get to
>   France. I found it through

enlistment in a Norton-Harjes
ambulance unit. A year before I
was to graduate, I sailed from New
York for the battlefront in France.
For six months, I drove a Ford
ambulance. I was in Picardy and at
Verdun. But an ambulance driver
was a noncombatant, not a fighter.
So I went to Paris and enlisted in
the French Foreign Legion, for
flight training at Tours. I was in
a squad of fifteen Americans.

                                                        CUT TO:

MONTAGE - Many chaotic scenes of World War I, including
trench warfare in France, in the desert in the Near East,
and war at sea. Overlying these scenes, scroll down the
names of those who appear later in the movie. In France:
Rex Benson, Stuart Menzies, Edward Wood (Lord Halifax),
William Donovan, Patrick Hurley, Winston Churchill, Gene
Markey, Col. Henry Stimson, Elizabeth "Betty" Crump, and
Sara Cunningham (later the wife of Cornelius Engert). In
the Middle East: Cornelius Engert, Edward "Fruity"
Metcalfe. At sea: Franklin Roosevelt (Assistant
Secretary of the Navy), Vincent Astor, Lord Mountbatten.
The last name to appear is Gordon Enders. Show images of
Gordon Enders and Betty Crump in their uniforms in 1919;
of Red Cross ambulances; of a military biplane (a French
Cauduron); film clips from "US AIR SERV RL1" accompanied
with Narration by A MAN WHO KNEW GORDON & BETTY ENDERS;
of U.S. Army General Hospital No. 9 in Chateauroux,
Brittany, France. And images of the Crump Label Factory
and Samuel Crump's mansion in Montclair, N.J.

                            GORDON ENDERS
One winter's day I came tumbling
out of the sky from three thousand
feet, near the little Brittany
village of Savenay. The left side
of my airplane had crumpled and I

had no parachute. I was reported dead; but days later, in a small local hospital, Elizabeth Crump found me alive. She was a Red Cross worker, whose duty it was, in her gray uniform with the blue tabs, to give razor blades and a score of other things to the wounded. She sat at the bedsides of the dying and wrote last messages home. She attended funerals and checked on the daily list of those reported dead, missing, and prisoners of war. I fell in love with her, and we were married in the Hotel de Ville in La Rochelle on April 22, 1919.

NARRATOR (V.O.)

ELIZABETH CRUMP ENDERS was the daughter of Samuel Crump, a wealthy inventor whose factories produced labels for canned goods. Samuel Crump and his wife, Anna Riker, lived in a mansion on Upper Mountain Boulevard, in Montclair, New Jersey. As a student of genealogy, their great-great granddaughter discovered that Elizabeth, known as Betty, and her brother, Samuel Crump III, were both in France in World War I. Sam, an Army lieutenant, was killed at the battle of Belleau Wood in September 1919, at age thirty.

A GREAT-NIECE OF BETTY ENDERS

Samuel Crump and Anna Riker had fifteen children. Only six

survived to adulthood. My grandmother, Julia Crump, was their youngest child. Betty was the eldest surviving daughter. She was born in May 1879, so she was 17 years older than Gordon. Betty was well equipped with her father's sense of business and personable enough by her own nature to win over customers and get the seamstresses on track to her high standards. Betty wrote about this in 1920:

ELIZABETH "BETTY" CRUMP ENDERS
Until the call of war brought my business activities to a sudden end, I was in charge of a bureau which I had organized six years previously and ran for a large dry goods store in New York City. It was named the College and School Bureau, and in connection with it, I carried on a large personal service work for the store. The work grew to large proportions, and is now a thoroughly established part of the organization. Previous experience, teaching in private schools, had given me an insight into the requirements of girls of this class and I now found this to be an invaluable asset.

A GREAT-NIECE OF BETTY ENDERS

The picture of Betty in her Red Cross uniform in 1919 shows her wearing a black arm band, in mourning for her brother Sam.

The next scenes and dialogue will be about the Three Men in a Jeep - Bromhead, Zimmermann, and Enders - from 1919-1941, in the period from WWI until the U.S enters WWII.

CUT TO:

MONTAGE - Scroll down as Narrator speaks, showing more images about Bromhead: Thurlby hall, Wellington College, Sandhurst, and file images of warfare in the desert of the Middle East. Show 3 ribbons and British General Service Medal (1918) with clasp for Iraq Campaign (1920), and medals for India Service (1908-35 and 1936) with clasps and oak leaf clusters for Waziristan (1921-24), North-West Frontier (1930), and Waziristan (1937). Then images of unspecified desert and mountains simulating Waziristan and Baluchistan, and scenes in Peshawar, showing Government House, Services Hotel, and Dean's Hotel. Medal and ribbon of the OBE at the conclusion; and images of Bromhead family, if they can be found.

NARRATOR (V.O.)

Benjamin Bromhead finished boarding school at Wellington College, and he entered the college-level program for British Army officers at Sandhurst. He then returned to central Asia, where as a junior officer, he fought in the Iraq Campaign of 1920. He then went to the North-West Frontier Province of India. He was wounded in the Waziristan Campaigns of 1922 and 1924. He was mentioned in despatches in fighting on the north-west Frontier in 1930. He became Sir Benjamin in July 1935, when his grandfather, Colonel Sir Benjamin Parnell Bromhead, the 4th Baronet, died. Sir Benjamin fought in the Waziristan Campaign in 1937 and was again mentioned in despatches. The next year, he married Nancy Lough of Buenos Aires. In 1940, soon after World War II broke out, he was given command of the Zhob Militia in Waziristan, along the border of Afghanistan. His troops prepared for a German invasion of India, in case Rommel reached the Suez Canal. Rommell's tanks would then have passed quickly across Asia to India. However, Rommel failed to reach Cairo. He was turned back by Montgomery at El-Alamein, and the Afrika Corps began its long retreat to the west. In 1943, Sir Benjamin was transferred to Peshawar, the capital of the North-West Frontier Province in India. He became the Assistant Political Agent in the office of the Governor. In November 1943, he and Lady Nancy and their two young daughters - one and three years old - were living at the Services Hotel in Peshawar. Nancy was pregnant with her third child. In 1943, Sir Benjamin Bromhead was invested with the "OBE," the Order of the British Empire.

CUT TO:

MONTAGE - Images in the life of Albert Zimmermann, scrolling down as V.O. Narrator speaks: High school and college. Marriage to Barbara Shoemaker, her parents (with Dr. Shoemaker in WWI uniform). Al & Barbara's home and social life, and their four children. His career in the fabric business (Artloom & Zimmermann's Sons) and wool business (Ott and Zimmermann). His experiences in secret intelligence arranged by his friend, Commander Jack Kane. At the appropriate moment, show Zimmermann's photographs for the FBI of the wedding of his maid, Anna, in Philadelphia in 1936, with swastikas on the armbands of the honor guard. Stills from movies taken by Zimmermann in Germany in 1937 showing Anna and her family after they returned to Germany, and of Nazi troops marching through Stuttgart.

NARRATOR (V.O.)

Al Zimmermann finished high school in Philadelphia. He then attended the University of Pennsylvania, where he received the Bachelor of Science in Mechanical Engineering, with honors, in 1923. His mother, Eva Kellenbenz, never learned English. She died in 1920, while Al was in college. He always spoke German with her. Al had a fine baritone voice, and he enjoyed performing solo and in small groups. He could accompany himself on the piano while talking with others. He learned to be wise, silent, and impassive as a member of the Sphinx Secret Society. He had a low handicap as a golfer and he was a good tennis player. His other skills included photography and making 16 millimeter home movies. In 1926, he married Barbara Shoemaker, a beautiful debutante who was the daughter of Philadelphia's leading eye surgeon. Al's father gave the newlyweds a wedding present of one million dollars, as he had done for each of his children. Zimmermann invested it wisely, and his father chose him to be his successor as an officer in both Zimmermann's Sons and Artloom. Al and Barbara Zimmermann moved to a new house that they built in Haverford, a suburb on Philadelphia's fashionable Main Line. They called their home "Cotswold Corners." Their first child, a daughter, was born in 1926, and then three more children – another daughter, born in 1929, and two sons, born in 1934 and 1937. Al joined the Orpheus Club, and was one of its star singers. He was also a member of the Merion Cricket Club, the Philadelphia Country Club, and the Fourth Street social Club. Barbara's best friend was the wife of Jack Kane, a Navy Reserve Commander who was the Deputy Director of Intelligence in Philadelphia for the 3rd Naval District. He was probably the person who asked Al to photograph the wedding of Al and Barbara's German maid in 1936, when the Nazi Bund acted as an honor guard at the church. The FBI took Zimmermann's pictures, and did not return them until after the war was over. In July 1937, Al and Barbara departed on a cruise to Europe on the S.S. Berengaria. They visited friends and business associates in England and Scotland. They then went to Holland, Germany, Austria, Italy, and France. In Stuttgart, they visited his mother's niece and also the couple whose marriage he photographed in Philadelphia in 1936; and they visited his aged

> aunt, who lived in the country near Stuttgart. Al took movies there that included several short segments, taken secretly, of Nazi troops marching through Stuttgart and of uniformed guards at street corners elsewhere in Germany.

The Narrator interrupts himself to introduce BARBARA SHOEMAKER ZIMMERMANN. He says, "Barbara Zimmermann wrote this in 1969 about their trip to Germany in 1937":

> BARBARA SHOEMAKER ZIMMERMANN
> In Stuttgart, we had dinner with Al's cousin who speaks very little English. I have accused Al, who claims to speak German, of talking baby talk as he learned it as a baby. No one seemed to understand him at first but he's improving and even I can understand a good deal. The cousin is very much opposed to Hitler although she wouldn't talk until we took her up to our room and then in decided undertones. [show stills from movies taken by Zimmermann] We then hired a car and drove to Gussenstad where Mr. Zimmermann was born eighty years ago. On the way back, we stopped to see an aunt, Mr. Z's sister, who lives in a cunning little cottage. Aunt Anna is a great Hitlerite, having lost everything during inflation, and now sitting pretty due to the Nazi regime. When we returned to Stuttgart, we had dinner with our former maid, Annie and her husband Paul. They are

> very happy and comfortable and are
> also strongly in favor of "Our
> Leader." His job is in an
> aeroplane factory.

>> CUT TO:

Images of FDR & Vincent Astor, the *Titanic*, and FDR's secret intelligence center, known as "The Room"; Zimmermann in blue navy uniform, his basic training class in DC; Admirals Harry Train and Zacharias, ONI headquarters at "Old Navy"; of Al's travel to India, showing a BOAC flying boat from Botwood, Newfoundland, to Limerick, Ireland; by C47 across North Africa; of Cairo, Shepheard's Hotel and the pyramids. Battle scenes representing Operation TORCH (North Africa, November 1942) and the invasion of Sicily (June 1943). Background music could include "As Time Goes By," from *Casablanca*.

> NARRATOR (V.O.)
> During the two years from 1937 to
> 1939, Al and Barbara Zimmermann
> watched as the Third Reich expanded
> its borders, incorporating Austria
> by "Anschluss," and Czechoslovakia,
> in spite of the false promise given
> by Hitler to Chamberlain, who said
> that it would yield "Peace in our
> time." They were therefore not
> surprised when in September 1939,
> Germany invaded Poland, and western
> Europe was again at war with
> Germany. Al had been carefully
> preparing for what he would do, if
> and when the U.S. entered the war.
> He had achieved success in his
> businesses – in the mills and his
> wool brokerage partnership – and he
> became a part-owner of the
> Philadelphia Phillies baseball
> team. The newspapers gave his

performance a better review in a Gilbert and Sullivan operetta in Philadelphia than the great baritone Nelson Eddy. From Jack Kane, he learned how provisional Naval Intelligence officers were recruited and selected. President Franklin Roosevelt had appointed his neighbor, Commander Vincent Astor, to vet all candidates on the east coast. In addition to Kane, Zimmermann had two other connections to Astor. One was his friend Jack Thayer, who had survived the sinking of the *Titanic* in 1912, when both Thayer's father and Astor's father went down with the ship. The other door-opener was his friend Malcolm Aldrich, known as "Mac." Aldrich was a cousin of Astor's good friend, the banker Winthrop Aldrich. And through his work as a wool broker, Zimmermann had contacts in many other countries, including India. In December 1941, after Pearl Harbor was attacked, Zimmermann wound up his work as a civilian, and in September 1942, at age 40, he was sworn in as a Naval Intelligence Officer. He went to Washington for basic training, although he already had the rank of Lieutenant. He learned there to function as a member of the Armed Forces, to think like a Navy man, and to behave like a Naval officer. He then went to basic intelligence school at Dartmouth College and advanced intelligence school in New York City. He learned how to use weapons, to handle secret documents, and to read and write in code. And he learned about the strange world of government secrets. After nine months of preparation, he was told that he would be sent to Karachi, India, as a Naval Liaison Officer. A few months later, he was promoted to be the senior U.S. Naval officer in that vital port city. While en route to Karachi, he passed through several port cities that had been freed from German occupation by the American-led invasion of North Africa in November 1942, code-named Operation TORCH. In Casablanca, he saw ruins that still remained from the battle. He recalled the movie *Casablanca*, which had been released in January 1943. When he arrived in Cairo, the first U.S. casualties were arriving from the invasion of Sicily. From Shepheard's Hotel in Cairo, Zimmermann wrote to his wife:

CUT TO:

Scenes of Gene Markey in Hollywood, his wives Joan Bennett and Hedy Lamarr; his movies & books; of Admiral Halsey and the battle for Guadalcanal, and of Lord Mountbatten and his headquarters as Supreme Commander in Asia in Kandy, Ceylon. And of Major Edward "Fruity" Metcalfe, who was coincidentally in Cairo when Zimmermann was there, although the two never met.

ZIMMERMANN
July 10, yesterday, I met the senior U.S. Naval intelligence officer for India, Commander Gene Markey, who is traveling to Delhi.

I was planning to visit Alexandria with Markey today, but we were ordered to stand by at the airport for travel to India.

     NARRATOR (V.O.)
Gene Markey led a double life, as a Hollywood producer, and as a Naval Intelligence Office. He was secretly a spy. At age 47, he was one of the notable figures in the "Golden Age of Hollywood." After Markey graduated from Dartmouth, he served as an Army lieutenant in France in World War I. He then studied at the Art Institute of Chicago, and he returned to California, where his wealthy father lived. He wrote books that were illustrated with his own portraits of famous authors and actors. He soon became famous himself, as he developed his skills as a screen writer and producer of many movies. One of his most notable films was *Wee Willie Winkie*, starring the famed Victor McLagen and with Shirley Temple in one of her first starring roles. It was directed by John Ford, who - like Markey - was already, secretly, in Naval Intelligence. Both men would become rear admirals after World War II. The movie *Wee Willie Winkie* was based on a fictional story by Rudyard Kipling. It was set along the border of Afghanistan, near Peshawar. This was the same area that would be traversed by Zimmermann and the others in Three Men in a Jeep.

Markey's other career - as a spy - began at Dartmouth, where, like Albert Zimmermann at the University of Pennsylvania, he belonged to the Sphinx secret society. In 1918, Markey was a second lieutenant at the Battles of Belleau Wood and Second Marne. He was promoted and decorated by both France and Italy, and in 1920, he quietly transferred from the Army to the Navy Reserve. He was ordered to active duty as a Naval Intelligence Officer before Pearl Harbor was attacked. He received the Bronze Star for leading an intelligence operation while serving on the staff of Admiral Halsey at the Battle for Guadalcanal. His frequent pre-war collaborator, John Ford, was also quietly active in the Navy Reserve before the war. He was wounded while filming the Battle of Midway. After the war was over, Markey co-produced and Ford directed the movie *In Harm's Way*, starring their friends John Wayne and Henry Fonda. Burgess Meredith played a role that simulated Markey, as a politically-connected Navy Reservist. Markey was promoted to captain after he and Zimmermann parted in Cairo. Gene Markey traveled between Delhi, India, and Kandy, Ceylon, as the U.S. Navy's Chief of Intelligence in the India-Burma area. While in Ceylon, he became a friend and trusted advisor to Lord Louis Mountbatten, Commander-in-Chief of the South-East Asia Command. He later wrote an authorized biography of Mountbatten. Markey had four wives. Before the war, Markey first married the actress Joan Bennett. After divorcing her, he married Hedy Lamarr, who was called "the most beautiful woman in the world." They were soon divorced. After the war, he married the actress Myrna Loy, with Admiral Halsey as his best man. After divorcing her, he married Lucille Wright, a wealthy widow who owned Calumet Farms and many winners of the Kentucky Derby. Admiral Markey then retired and lived the life of a very wealthy country gentleman.

CUT TO:

A B-24, simulating a flight across Asia to Iraq and Karachi; scenes of Naval Liaison Office, Karachi, and of Navy and civilians at the NLO & elsewhere in Karachi

NARRATOR (V.O.)
King Edward VIII's former equerry, Major Edward Metcalfe, known as "Fruity" Metcalfe, was also in Cairo at the time that Zimmermann was there, although they would not have had a reason to meet. Nor could they have imagined that 45 years later, Metcalfe's grandson would marry Zimmermann's granddaughter. They met when they were students at Yale. [pause] "Fruity" Metcalfe met Edward when he was Prince of Wales, on a tour of India. His job was to find suitable women in India to satisfy the prince's well-known search for pleasure. Edward's correspondence

with Metcalfe mentions "that bitch in Peshawar." Metcalfe was married to "Baba" Curzon, daughter of Lord George Curzon, who was formerly a Viceroy of India. "Fruity" Metcalfe was also a friend of Lieutenant-Colonel Rex Benson, who was with him in India in the 1930s. In Washington, D.C., in 1941, it was Benson who wrote a card of introduction for Gordon Enders to present in Peshawar, India, to the Governor of the North-West Frontier Province. This was the first step in what later became the journey of Three Men in a Jeep.
[pause]
Zimmermann flew from Cairo to India in an R.A.F. B-24 "Liberator." The pilot let him fly the plane for a while. After he arrived in India, he wrote to his wife:

AL ZIMMERMANN
Karachi at last. Got up at three to leave at day break. Arrived here at 0130 but it was 0500 Karachi time. I didn't need the parachute so I didn't find out whether it worked or not. They say you can always get another if it doesn't.

NARRATOR (V.O.)
In the meantime, BARBARA SHOEMAKER ZIMMERMANN was at home with their four children. In September 1943, she was lonesome, worried, and cold. She wrote about her feelings in an article published in *Vogue* magazine.

BARBARA ZIMMERMANN
My husband is a fighting force some 12,000 miles away on the other side of the world, and I'm not a brave little woman. My four children and I are making the necessary adjustments, and we are managing to retain a slight vestige of humor. And that we don't think longingly of life before the war. Yesterday the thermometer fluctuated between 44 and 48 degrees. In September, mind you! I prefer living with my husband right here with me, and I don't care who knows it. I'm proud of him, but I want him back home, and soon!

CUT TO:

Gordon and Betty Crump Enders in 1920-1937, with their comments read aloud as V.O.'s by actors who read from their books, interspersed with narrator's V.O. The covers and title pages of their four books are shown, and images are shown during the V.O., showing scenes in China and Tibet taken by them, and Google images showing locations in America and Asia.

NARRATOR (V.O.)
Soon after Gordon Enders and Betty Crump were married in France, they returned to America. They visited her family, and also his family in Pennsylvania. In 1920, Betty showed her independent spirit and her skill as a writer. She wrote that to be a successful businesswoman,

BETTY ENDERS
There's no trick to it. Just use your common sense. Then have the courage to carry out your plan.

NARRATOR (V.O.)
In 1920, Gordon studied for the examination to become an assistant attaché for the U.S. Department of Commerce in China. It seems very likely that he was also recruited and trained at that time to be a secret intelligence officer for the U.S. Government. Enders wrote:

GORDON ENDERS
I had barely set foot in America when I found myself headed for Asia, as a representative of the United States Department of Commerce in Shanghai and Peking. My ultimate objective was to complete my picture of Tibet and the Grand Lamas, and to find out whether there was any place for me to use the specialized knowledge which Chanti had so diligently implanted. My immediate objective was to act as secretary to the commercial attaché and to master the diplomatic details of trade promotion, information, and protection. I was an American delegate at the sessions of the important Tariff Revision Commission at Shanghai, and I participated in efforts to untangle the Japanese-American wireless imbroglio. It was my first personal contact with the Japanese spy system. Our suitcase was stolen, and then several months later it was mysteriously returned. The envelope containing our diplomatic code showed that it had been

steamed open and then carefully resealed. For months we had been operating with a code which was as easy for the Japanese to read as if our messages had been sent in plain English. [pause] During my period of official service in Peking I met most of the important figures of Chinese life of that day. My wife was keenly interested in the life of the Chinese women and made many friends among them. In 1923 I left government service and went into business in Shanghai. News came that the Panchan Lama was leaving Tibet for a voluntary exile in China. Nowhere else in the world could the things have happened which took place in China during the years that followed.

NARRATOR (V.O.)
Gordon and Betty Enders returned to America in 1923, but within months, they went back to China. Gordon became the agent for several American companies. They traveled widely on business and for adventure throughout China. They returned to America from time to time, but they spent most of the years from 1923 until 1937 in China. In 1923, Betty wrote:

BETTY ENDERS
Our voyage to China had been mostly sunshine and warm days, blue skies and bluer seas; and now before us lay the beauties of the Inland Sea. To my husband, who I called "Pierre," I lazily remarked, "none

but a poet with a burning soul could do justice to this heavenly spot!" Pierre was looking through his glasses and did not answer, but I knew that he, too, was touched by the spell. Pierre's work kept him closely confined these days, so with my private rickshaw boy I explored Shanghai.

              NARRATOR (V.O.)
Gordon and Betty Enders returned to China in 1923. Betty's father, Samuel Crump, soon came for a visit. He suddenly became ill and died there in September 1925 at the age of 83. By this time, the country was in turmoil. Endless fighting was taking place between local warlords and relatives of the last emperor of China. And to complicate matters, Japan had been taking stock of the troubled situation in China ever since its victory against Russia in 1906. In 1931, it staged the "Mukden Incident," which was the pretext for the Japanese invasion of China. Meanwhile, in 1923, Gordon learned to speak and write in Mandarin while he was in Peking, now called Beijing. Gordon and Betty traveled widely throughout China until 1937, sometimes together and sometimes separately. They wrote four books about their years in China, which are illustrated with his photographs. Her books overlap with his in some instances, and they tell some of the same stories from her point of view. She called

him "Pierre," perhaps recalling the ribald joke about "Lucky Pierre, the amorous French fighter pilot," which was often told by veterans of World War I. They returned to the U.S. several times between 1923 and 1937. Gordon sold 20 Corsair bombers to the Nationalist air force of Chiang Kai-shek, and he trained the pilots to use them. He also became the personal pilot for Generalissimo and Madame Chiang. Enders was introduced by the Chiangs to the 9th Panchan Lama, of Tashilumpo Monastery, who was then the ruler of Tibet. Britain and Russia had long competed for power in Tibet, as part of "the Great Game" between those two empires. The Panchan Lama believed that China should be the protector of Tibet, as it had been in the distant past. With the Chiang's blessing, the Panchan made Enders one of his most trusted advisors, and he appointed him to be Senator in the Tibetan government, with a "Golden Passport." No other Westerner, before or since, has ever had such an official position in Tibet. The Panchan employed Enders to fly many tons of gold dust from Tibet to Shanghai, in China. The Panchan's gold was intended to pay for Chiang's protection of Tibet. It was to fund the Panchan's vision of a "New Heart of Asia" in Tibet. The Panchan's dream ended suddenly when he died on a trip back to Tibet in 1937. The leadership of Tibet then passed from the Monastery of Tashilumpo to the Potala in Lhasa, and to the followers of the 14th Dalai Lama. He was born in 1935 as Tenzin Gyatso. And he is still alive - the world-famous "Dalai Lama" - who fled from Tibet to India in 1959. He was only two years old in 1937, and until 1950, when he became of age, the Tibetan government in Lhasa was under the control of officials and monks of the Dalai Lama. They were not interested in a cooperative relationship with China. The Panchan's vision for cooperation by Tibet and China then quietly faded away. And at the same time - in 1937 - the Japanese invasion force reached Shanghai. Betty Enders had previously returned to America. Gordon joined in the defense of Shanghai, and he barely escaped to the U.S. when the city fell. Gordon wrote about it in his book, *Foreign Devil*, published in 1942:

GORDON ENDERS
I returned to Shanghai before the fighting reached that metropolitan city. I stayed just off Avenue Joffre, between the Avenue du Roi Albert and Rue Cardinal Mercier. Within less than a month's time the fighting moved down to Shanghai. The city rocked to the sound of bursting air bombs, naval artillery, machine guns, and hand grenades. By the first week in September, it became evident that Shanghai would fall to the

>   Japanese. The night was dark and
>   the road to the riverside dock was
>   jammed with war traffic and
>   slippery with mud. My wartime
>   driving experience in France stood
>   me in good stead, and I returned to
>   America.

                              CUT TO:

London, New Year's Day, 1936. Show exterior of a
magnificent house in Belgravia, near Buckingham Palace;
and of a grand interior, with a formal dinner party and a
small orchestra.

                    NARRATOR (V.O.)
>   Reginald Benson, known as Rex, and
>   later as Sir Rex Benson, was head
>   of the largest private bank in
>   England. He was married to an
>   American, Leslie Foster – formerly
>   the wife of Condé Nast. On the
>   evening of New Year's Day in 1936,
>   at their home in London, they
>   hosted a dinner party in honor of
>   Edward, Prince of Wales. Rex
>   Benson was a cousin by marriage of
>   Stuart Menzies. Both of them were
>   wounded and decorated in World War
>   I, and they were both deeply
>   involved with secret British
>   intelligence operations. Menzies
>   later became head of MI-6, the
>   Secret Intelligence Service. In
>   1941, as a lieutenant-colonel, Rex
>   Benson was sent to become the
>   Military Attaché in the British
>   embassy in Washington. Benson had
>   served in India as a young officer.
>   He was in Peshawar when the Prince
>   of Wales visited that city with his

equerry, Edward "Fruity" Metcalfe. Their correspondence suggests that "Fruity" pimped for the Prince, who was a notorious womanizer. "Fruity" later married Alexandra "Baba" Curzon, who was born when her father was Viceroy of India.
[pause]
The published guest list at Benson's party on January 1, 1936, shows that the Prince's lover, Wallis Simpson was there. And also, Duff Cooper, the war minister (later Viscount Norwich), and his wife Lady Diana; Sir Robert Vansittart, permanent head of the Foreign Office, and his wife; "Foxy" Gwynne, a rich man-about-town; and Johnny McMullen, a writer for *Vogue* and a close friend of both Mrs. Simpson and Mrs. Benson. Benson's friend "Fruity" Metcalfe and his wife "Baba" Curzon were probably there, too. And probably also the Prince's friend Lord Halifax, formerly Viceroy of India. Lord Halifax famously defended the Nazi-leaning actions of Edward VIII. Rex Benson's work with MI-6 included keeping careful watch on Edward, both as Prince and King, to ensure that he wouldn't jump ship and join the Nazis. At the Bensons' party, the Prince enjoyed himself so much that he and Mrs. Simpson stayed until 1:45 a.m. on January 2; and with Benson at the piano, they danced "all the popular airs." Prince Edward's father, King George V, died 18 days later, and the Prince became King Edward

>VIII. After King Edward abdicated on December 11, 1936, he was made Duke of Windsor. And then as Duke of Winsor, he married Wallis Simpson in 1937. After Britain declared war on Germany in 1939, Benson was ordered to increase his watch over the Duke of Winsor, who continued to enjoy his Nazi friends. The Duke and Duchess were sent to the Bahamas in July 1940, and he finished the war there as governor. Halifax was sent to Washington in January 1941. He was the British ambassador there when Benson was the Military Attaché.

CUT TO:

Resume the story of Gordon and Betty Enders from 1937-1941. Scenes showing Poughkeepsie, N.Y.; Lafayette, Indiana; Chautauqua, N.Y.; Washington, DC - and locations in the Pacific & India, as they appear in the narration. Introduce Eleanor Roosevelt, Ambassador Louis Dreyfus, Deputy Secretary of State Sumner Welles; Cornelius Van H. Engert and his wife Sara. Reappearing: Secretary of War Henry Stimson, General Patrick Hurley, Lt-Col. Rex Benson, Ambassador Lord Halifax, and Bob Enders.

> NARRATOR (V.O.)
> After visiting Gordon Enders' brother Bob and their mother in Pennsylvania, and Betty's parents in Poughkeepsie, Gordon and Betty Enders moved to Indiana, where Gordon became a professor of history at Purdue University. Betty was a distant relative of the president of the university. They both had the opportunity to travel widely in America, and they used the Redpath Agency in Chicago to

negotiate contracts for their speeches. Gordon was a popular lecturer about the dangerous situation in the Far East, and Betty told fascinating stories about her adventures in China. She was on the Chautauqua Lecture Circuit with Eleanor Roosevelt, and they often lectured at the same places. Early in 1941, it became clear to both Gordon and Betty that the U.S. would soon be at war in the Pacific. Japan had taken over the Asian colonies of France and the Netherlands, after the surrender of those countries to the Germans. Japan knew that Britain could not provide security for its empire in Asia, and the Philippines and other U.S. territories were vulnerable to a Japanese attack. Gordon indicated his willingness to return to active duty in the Army, and in September 1941, he was commissioned as a major in G-2, the Army Intelligence branch. He would be sent to Kabul, Afghanistan, as the Military Attaché, to become the first American diplomat ever stationed in Afghanistan. He would also have collateral duty as the senior U.S. Army intelligence officer for the entire country of India, a position called Military Observer. The unusual and sensitive nature of this assignment makes it highly likely that he was interviewed and briefed in the War Department - probably by the Secretary of War, Colonel Henry Stimson, and perhaps also by

Patrick Hurley, a former Secretary of War – and by the State Department, probably by Sumner Welles, the Deputy Secretary. Gordon would see General Hurley again in Kabul in 1944. The meeting in Washington would have been in the State, War, and Treasury Building, now known as the Eisenhower Executive Office Building. Enders would also have been given information from the diplomat who was then responsible for Afghanistan, Louis Goethe Dreyfus, who was on home leave from his position as Minister in Tehran, Iran. Dreyfus would be his mentor in diplomatic affairs, and Enders had additional duty as Dreyfus' assistant military attaché. Only two years later, Dreyfus would be tasked with organizing the Tehran Conference, at which time FDR and Churchill met with Stalin. Dreyfus would have told Enders about the man who was expected soon to be named by FDR as the head of the U.S. Mission in Afghanistan: Cornelius Engert – who had a reputation in the State Department as a brilliant but conniving career Foreign Service Officer, who had acquired a well-deserved reputation for dishonesty. Nevertheless, Engert and his wife, the former Sara Cunningham, a socialite from San Francisco, had won the confidence of President Roosevelt and his wife. It is possible that Gordon and Betty Enders met Cornelius and Sara Engert at this

time. Perhaps at the British embassy, where they could have been introduced by Dreyfus; and where Gordon could also have met his British counterpart as a military attaché, Colonel Rex Benson, and perhaps also the Ambassador, Lord Halifax. We know that Benson gave him a card of introduction to present to Sir George Cunningham, governor of the North-West Frontier Province, at his residence in Peshawar. Enders presented the card from Benson when he saw the governor in December 1941 as he was about to cross the Khyber Pass into Afghanistan.   [pause]
In theory, Enders would now have two masters: The War Department, and the Department of State. In fact, he operated on his own, often without orders or restraint. He needed no additional training to do this. [pause] Within a month, Enders flew west from Washington across the Pacific with several high-ranking Army officers. In November 1941, they were sent to be in place in various locations in Asia at the time of the expected Japanese attack on the territories of the U.S. and Britain in the Far East. Their trip took them to Delhi, India, via Hawaii and the Philippines, and then carefully, using British airfields, probably Hong Kong and Singapore - avoiding territory controlled by Japan - to Calcutta. They must have stopped for fuel at Midway Island, Wake Island, and Guam. Within two

>   months, all of these locations in
>   the Pacific would all be attacked.
>   Wake and Guam would fall to Japan.

                                                        CUT TO:

Enders writes about his trip across India from Calcutta
by train to Delhi and to Peshawar, and by auto into
Afghanistan (November - December 1941). Show images of
India in the 1940s, the Himalayas, Calcutta, Delhi, the
Grand Trunk Road, Gen. Raymond A. Wheeler, General (later
Field Marshal) Archibald Wavell and his family, Peshawar,
Sir George Cunningham, the Khyber Pass, Hindu Kush
Mountains, and other scenes described by Enders.

>   NARRATOR (V.O.)
>   Starting in mid-November 1941,
>   Enders typed letters to his wife as
>   he traveled across India. Every
>   day or two for the next two weeks,
>   he sent letters to Betty. He meant
>   for her to share them with their
>   families, and he hoped that they
>   also might be used in broadcasts
>   from the radio station at Purdue
>   University. Some excerpts follow,
>   narrated by Enders:
>
>   GORDON ENDERS
>   Last night - it was November 17 -
>   before taking the train, I had
>   dinner at the Farbos, an Italian-
>   owned restaurant which is
>   considered the best in Calcutta. I
>   took the 9:03 train and had a very
>   comfortable two-bunk compartment to
>   myself. I am drinking in the
>   Hindustan that I knew 30 years ago.
>   The grand trunk road is now paved,
>   and there are Hindu and Mohammedan

restaurants at the big stations. We stopped to take our lunch at Fatehpur-Haswa, where my father is buried. I caught a glimpse of the great peepul tree in the monkey temple yard. [pause] On November 20, we reached Delhi. This morning I drove out to call on the local Afghan consul general. My object was to show him my passport and let him know my plans. The consul general is young, and quite handsome, speaking excellent English. I'm told that Afghanistan wants an American official and I was pleased with the whole atmosphere of our talk. [pause] It's now Saturday, November 22. In a few minutes I must dress to have dinner with General Sir Archibald Wavell. It's to be with General Wheeler and his party, some of whom I met in Washington and some in Honolulu. [long pause] I <u>greatly</u> enjoyed the dinner. There were about fifteen - three of us were Americans. Lady Wavell sat opposite her husband at the center of the long table, and I was placed at her left. After dinner I talked with General Wavell. [pause] It's now November 26. I'll leave here tomorrow morning and it will take me twenty-four hours to reach Peshawar. Yesterday I bought warm blankets, extra warm clothing, and a steel trunk. [pause] I'm now at Dean's Hotel in Peshawar. It's Saturday, November 29. I'm all set to cross the border into Afghanistan on Wednesday or

> Thursday of next week. In Delhi I sat in a conference with our General Wheeler and British G.H.Q. and have received what are practically orders to drive up to Russia and into Iran and down to the Indian border again. It's about 2000 miles. [pause] After tiffin on December 1, we took a car and drove to the Kabul River, which is in tribal territory about 14 miles from here. We were always in sight of the big peak, Tatarar, behind which lies the Khyber Pass and Afghanistan. I will have dinner tomorrow with the governor, Sir George Cunningham, to whom I carry Colonel Benson's letter of introduction. [pause] It's now December 2. After lunch with the local R.A.F. acting chief and his wife, I dressed for the Governor's dinner. There were Lady and Sir George Cunningham, four others, and myself. My after-dinner talk with him was most informative and helpful.

Images are scrolled down to show places and people mentioned by the Narrator from 1941-1943, including U.S. Chargé d'affaires Charles Thayer, U.S. Minister Cornelius Engert and his family, British Ambassador Sir Francis Wylie, and Italian Ambassador Pietro Quaroni. Maps of central Asia and Afghanistan appear with red dots and boundary lines to show, as they appear in V.O.: Tehran, Jalalabad, Kabul, Uzbekistan, Tajikistan, the Wakhan peninsula, Herat, Kandahar and Helmand province, Quetta, and Nuristan - the land of Kipling's "The Man Who Would Be King." Add map and images of India and Tibet, Lhasa, British Secretary of State for India Sir Olaf Caroe, Col. Suydam Cutting, Major Ilya Tolstoy, Captain Brooke Dolan, and the 14th Dalai Lama. Most of these can be found in *"Dearest Barb" from Karachi, 1943-1945.*

                NARRATOR (V.O.)
Enders left for the Khyber Pass to cross into Afghanistan on Saturday, December 6, for the two-day drive to Kabul. Coincidentally, he arrived in Kabul on December 8, the day that Pearl Harbor was attacked (Asia time). He was the only American diplomat in Afghanistan for the next five months. At the time he arrived, the prevailing view in the Afghan government was that the Germans would win the war; that Britain was barely surviving; and the Nazis would soon take Stalingrad and Moscow. Although Afghanistan officially remained neutral, it wanted be aligned with the winning side. It took all of Enders' skills to convince the Afghans that the Allies, now led by America, would turn the tide and win the war. With his sensibility for Asian cultures and his gift for languages, Enders soon became popular with the Afghans.
Following General Wheeler's orders in Delhi, he traveled widely in his jeep from Kabul: north to River Oxus, now known as the Amu Darya, on the border of Afghanistan with Uzbekistan and Tajikistan in the Soviet Union; to the Wakhan Peninsula in the north-east; to the ancient Persian city of Herat in the west; back to Jalalabad and Nuristan in the southeast; and in

the southwest into the Helmand
Province to Kandahar, Afghanistan,
and then crossing the Border to
Quetta, India. There were no paved
roads in Afghanistan at that time,
and the countryside was famously
lawless. But he could speak both
Pashto and Persian, and he soon
learned the other dialects of the
country, and he boldly confronted
anyone who tried to stand in his
way.
 [pause]
With his diplomatic passport and
military credentials, Enders could
in theory cross the Border between
India and Afghanistan at any time
or place. He undoubtedly returned
to Peshawar in mid-February 1942 to
meet his former mentor, Chiang Kai-
shek, when the Generalissimo
visited the Governor and went to
the Khyber Pass. Chiang's visit was
kept secret until he returned to
Delhi on February 15.

[photos of Chiang's trip to India are on Google images]

In May 1942, Enders went to Tehran,
Iran, to escort Charles Thayer, the
newly-appointed Chargé d'Affaires,
to Kabul. Thayer was a cousin of
Zimmermann's friend Jack Thayer,
who survived the sinking of
Titanic; and he was a brother of
Zimmermann's good friend George
Thayer. Charles Thayer was thus
probably responsible for selecting
Zimmermann to join Enders and
Bromhead on their trip in November

1943. Thayer was a West Point graduate. He later was an O.S.S. officer in Yugoslavia, and he ended his government career as Head of the Voice of America. He and Enders got along well, especially after they spent two harrowing weeks together, fighting their way through mountains and bandit country from Tehran to Kabul. Their trip included having their tires shot out and crashing into a river. Enders and Thayer soon found a place in Kabul for the U.S. Minister Cornelius and Sara Engert and their two children to live. The American Legation was officially opened with the arrival of the Engerts in June 1942.
          [pause]
Over the next 18 months, the Chief of Mission, Cornelius Engert, was often irritated by Enders, who acted as if Engert was not his superior. Engert wrote angry inter-office memos to Enders, and, to no avail, he also complained about Enders to both the State Department and to U.S. military officers in Delhi. Engert and Enders also differed in their relationships with other diplomats in Kabul. Engert, who later received Britain's O.B.E., was close to the British Ambassador, Sir Francis Wylie. You might say that he "sucked up" to Wylie. Major Enders, on the other hand, thought Wylie was pompous and inept. The Italian Ambassador, Pietro Quaroni, agreed. After

Italy surrendered and switched sides in the war, Quaroni implied that Wylie, proud in his elegant red jacket with decorations, and also the Germans, who strutted in their black uniforms, failed to recognize that the Afghans privately laughed at them behind their backs. CHARLES THAYER wrote to the State Department, saying:

THAYER
Fortunately for the Axis, every blunder it made was balanced by another made by the British. After the Italians surrendered to the Allies and switched sides in the war, Quaroni told me that "Every night I went to bed, I thanked God for Sir Francis Wylie." The British habit of warning the Afghans of every petty intrigue among their own subjects constantly irritated the Afghan government. Probably the worst blunder of the British was the expulsion of the Axis nationals in 1941. Quaroni says he told Pilger, the German Minister, that, "had it not been for this mistake, the Axis Legations would have been closed by the Afghans in June 1942 because of the blatant and clumsy intriguing of the Axis colony." Quaroni also said that he believed that the British and Americans should assure the Afghans that the Russians had not been given a free hand in Central Asia at the Moscow Conference.

NARRATOR (V.O.)
The Afghans also took note as the tide of war slowly shifted in favor of the Allies, led by the United States. In February 1942, the U.S. won a surprise victory over the Japanese at the Battle of Midway. Then in November 1942, Rommel was pushed back from Cairo, and the Afrika Korps retreated west across North Africa. In the same month, the Allies landed at Casablanca, and other ports in western North Africa. Three months later, in February 1943, the Russians finally defeated the Germans at Stalingrad, and in the same month, in the Pacific, the U.S. took back Guadalcanal from the Japanese. The success of the U.S. invasion of Sicily in July 1943 was expected to be followed by an Allied attack on the mainland of Italy. British forces landed at the "toe of Italy" on 3 September 1943, and the surrender of Italy was announced five days later. But the Afghans foresaw continued British meddling in their affairs, and they rightly feared that success of the U.S.S.R. would enable Russia to subvert Afghanistan's independence. Afghanistan expected that it would again become the focus of the Great Game, and it hoped the U.S. would play an impartial role as peace maker between these two Great Powers.
[pause]
However, little was known at that time of President Franklin

Roosevelt's long-standing plan to insert America into the power struggle in Central Asia. In FDR's most recent effort in this plan, early in 1942 he directed General William Donovan to send two O.S.S. officers - Major Ilya Tolstoy and Captain Brooke Dolan - to travel to New Delhi, and then to Lhasa, Tibet, to present gifts to the young 14th Dalai Lama. One of the gifts was a signed photograph of FDR in a silver frame. The British were uneasy about American interference in what they considered their territorial affairs. Grudging permission was finally given by Sir Olaf Caroe, Foreign Secretary in the government of India. Roosevelt's old classmate and wealthy friend, Col. Suydam Cutting, now in the O.S.S. in Delhi, paved the way with Caroe, and permission was granted for the O.S.S. team to proceed in the summer of 1942. They met the 10-year old Dalai Lama in December 1942. The Tibetans asked for a powerful radio, which alarmed the Chinese government. The O.S.S. team was withdrawn in March 1943.

FADE TO:

Naval Liaison Office, Karachi, 19 July 1943. Images of Karachi scroll down and the following people are introduced: Lieutenant Commander Howard Smith, British Intelligence Officer John (J.R.) Harris, U.S. Consul Clarence Macy, Lady Vere Birdwood, Alice Swayne-Thomas, Lieutenant Curtin Winsor, and Commodore Milton Miles. CORNELIUS ENGERT speaks. Captain Gene Markey reappears.

NARRATOR (V.O.)
Zimmermann was soon caught up in the web of intelligence work. He was assigned to write a report about the Port of Karachi, and he completed it in the fall of 1943. His 50-page report is preserved in the National Archives. It is still marked with the notation, "to be copied only with permission from the Secretary of the Navy." Zimmermann learned to work and socialize with the leaders of the British community in Karachi, including Sir Hugh Dow, Governor of Sind Province; the Governor's *aide de camp*; important civilians (some of whom he had business dealings with before the war); and high-ranking officers in the British Army and Navy. He played bridge, tennis, and golf with wives of officers who were on detached duty elsewhere in India, including April Swayne-Thomas and Lady Vere Birdwood. There was nothing romantic about these games, but his wife couldn't help but wonder and worry. He became a close friend of the American consul general, Clarence Macy, and he worked closely with the British Intelligence Officer in Karachi, John Harris. He became wary of his commanding officer, Lieutenant Commander Howard Smith. Zimmermann discovered that his commander had learned the lessons of how to succeed in the Orient, using *cumshaw* (picking up anything unattended), *baksheesh* (tipping and

bribing) and "squeeze" (threats and pressure).

ZIMMERMANN
The night I arrived in Karachi a Russian lady by the name of Dubash was here for dinner. She was married to a Parsi Indian who died about a year ago. She's quite attractive, I would say pushing fifty.

NARRATOR (V.O.)
Two weeks later, Zimmermann wrote:

ZIMMERMANN
We had a dinner for eight, including the British commander in Karachi - General and Mrs. Hind, and Mrs. Dubash - whom I mentioned before, Commander Smith and myself. After dinner Mrs. Dubash played on the piano - mostly Russian songs - and I took a whack at a song on the banjo.

NARRATOR (V.O.)
By October 1943, Zimmermann referred to Nadia Dubash as the Commander's "girl friend." In February 1944, Smith was relieved (that is to say, removed) as Commanding Officer, with an unsatisfactory fitness report, and Zimmermann was placed in charge. Zimmermann was directed by Lieutenant CURTIN WINSOR in the Office of Naval Intelligence in Washington to:

CURTIN WINSOR
Eliminate counter intelligence activities and discharge Sheikh, and discharge Madame Dubash, too.

NARRATOR (V.O.)
It appears that Commander Smith had been dipping into the funds allocated to the Naval Liaison Office, and there may also have been a *menage a trois* involving Smith, Sheikh and Madame Dubash. Smith's ability as a consummate cumshaw artist would later be useful for Commodore Milton Miles, who was the senior U.S. Navy officer in China. The commodore was not to be trifled with, having been personally selected for his job in China by the Chief of Naval Operations, Admiral Ernest King. Zimmermann, in Karachi, and Winsor, in Washington, had to be very careful as they played in the ruthless game of high-level Navy politics.

[pause]

Zimmermann's assignment to travel along the North-West Frontier had probably been under consideration for several months. It may have been the reason that he was selected to go to Karachi, or it may have been suggested by Gene Markey after the two men met in Cairo. We recall that both men were members of the same secret society, Sphinx. Zimmermann's assignment to go on the Trip along the Border of the north-west frontier was approved by Charles

Thayer in Kabul. Charles Thayer was the brother of Zimmermann's good friend George Thayer. There are also good reasons that an American Naval officer would have been assigned to accompany Enders on this trip. The U.S. Navy had a long-standing interest in having secure ports around the world, and ports on the Indian Ocean were thus vital to the Navy. The Navy was especially interested in the port of Karachi, at the outlet of the Indus River. Zimmermann's very thorough report on the port of Karachi in September 1943 had caught the attention of his superiors in Washington. The port of Karachi was protected from Russia by the country of Afghanistan, and by its southern border with India - now Pakistan. The trip by Enders and Zimmermann along the North-West Frontier's border was intended to introduce America to the complex reality of the situation along the Border. In addition, Gordon Enders had developed a reputation for exaggeration, so it would be good to have another observer who could record what was heard and seen. Zimmermann was considered to be very bright, and he was perfect for the assignment. "4.0 Zimmermann" was his nick-name in Intelligence school - and he had proved his ability to be a good photographer, recorder, and observer. [pause]
On October 26, 1943, Zimmermann was visited by the British Central

Intelligence Officer in Karachi, JOHN R. HARRIS, Esquire, who read him a letter from Intelligence Bureau Quetta. The letter was marked "Express - Secret and Personal." He gave Zimmermann a copy of the letter.

           J. R. HARRIS

Dear John,
I have just heard from Major Sir Benjamin Bromhead of the North-West Frontier Province Public Relations Bureau that with the blessing of the Governor N.W.F.P. he is taking Major Enders, U.S. Military Attaché, Kabul, on a personally conducted tour of the Frontier and Baluchistan from Chitral to Quetta with the idea of making it clear to the American Legation in Kabul what are our frontier problems and our ideas and policy in dealing with them and the Afghans. I promptly asked him whether he could also take one of the American officers from the U.S. Naval Liaison Office if they would like to send one. He replied in the affirmative, subject to the Governor's sanction. Would you put the offer to Smith and ask him to telegraph me a reply, saying whether they would like to send an officer, and if so whom. This would be a somewhat unique opportunity of getting a first-class background for his own office and Naval H.Qs at Washington to use in connection with any reports emanating from U.S. sources in Kabul or Delhi. You will readily

appreciate the necessity for carefully picking the officer so that he does not get hold of the wrong end of the stick or miss important points. How Smith would explain to Enders and Engert the presence of this officer would be Smith's headache and not ours! The weather will be bitterly cold with the possibility of snow in Waziristan and Chitral, so warm clothes are essential. Bromhead's dates are 18 November, leave Peshawar for Chitral; 25 November, return to Peshawar; 29 November, leave for Waziristan; 10 December, finish tour in Quetta. It means a month away from the Naval Office in Karachi.

          NARRATOR (V.O.)
Zimmermann was promptly chosen to make the trip with Bromhead and Enders, probably as a result of heavy pressure exerted on Commander Smith by Harris. In less than a week, Zimmermann was sent as a courier to U.S. Naval Headquarters in Colombo, Ceylon, where he undoubtedly received instructions on what to look for and what to be wary of on the Frontier. He flew to Ceylon on 31 October and spent two days and a night there. The Senior Naval Intelligence Officer in the South-East Asia Theater, Captain Gene Markey, was probably there to give him instructions. Zimmermann returned via Bombay and was back in Karachi on 3 November. Five days later, he was given

orders to go to Peshawar, signed by Smith. He studied them carefully.

                ZIMMERMANN

"Subject: Temporary Additional Duty. On or about 11 November 1943, you will proceed via transportation furnished by the United States Army, to Peshawar, North West Frontier Province, India, and <u>such other places as may be deemed necessary for the proper performance of the duties assigned you</u>. [emphasis added] Upon completion of this temporary duty you will return to this office and resume your regular duties. You are authorized to defray any additional travel subject to reimbursement by the government."

                NARRATOR (V.O.)

We can imagine what Zimmermann was thinking as he read these orders: "After I reach Peshawar, can I go anywhere and do anything that I believe is consistent with what I have been told in Ceylon? And then come back to Karachi when it's over? It looks like a license to do <u>anything</u> that I believe is necessary. [musing] Umm!! I need to keep a careful record of this trip." [underlines are added for emphasis]

Outline of the next three weeks: Zimmermann travels by train from Karachi to Peshawar. He meets Bromhead at the railroad station in Peshawar, and he socializes in this ancient city. He and Bromhead visit the Tribal Area near

Peshawar. Enders arrives in his jeep, "Ma Kabul," a day later than expected. The Three Men then travel along the border of Afghanistan to Chitral, crossing over the Lowari pass. After a short stay in Chitral, they go over the Lowari again and return to Peshawar. Enders vanishes for three days, while Zimmermann writes his notes, socializes, and visits the Khyber Pass. Later the same afternoon, Enders reappears, and the Three Men come to a garden party at the Governor's house. They are debriefed by the Viceroy, General Wavell, with Enders doing most of the talking. The three officers then go on the second part of their journey along the Afghan border. It is a harrowing trip through Waziristan to Quetta. They are accompanied by armed guards, with armored vehicles leading the way, and also following them. Zimmermann mentions episodes of random gunfire, bombings by the R.A.F., and fatal accidents to other vehicles along the road. The Three Men go separate ways as they leave Quetta. Enders goes back by his jeep, "Ma Kabul," to Kabul, Bromhead travels by armored car to Peshawar, and Zimmermann returns to Karachi by train. Narrator's V.O. alternates with Zimmermann, reading from his notes, the titles and legends that he wrote on his photographs, and letters to his wife, Barbara.

Illustrations simultaneously scroll down during V.O., to show Zimmermann's photos and a few photos taken by Bromhead; short segments of Zimmermann's movies; and file photos from Google images and the internet of scenes in the script.

                    ZIMMERMANN
Wednesday, November 10. Day after
tomorrow I leave for the North West
Frontier by Indian train. It will
take 48 hours to get there, and I
expect to be away about a month.
[pause]
November 12. The first part to
Lahore was in an air-conditioned
car. I shared a compartment with a

Colonel Fagin who knows a friend of ours. From Lahore on it was a bit different - no luxuries at all. I was supposed to be in Class I but it was nearer III. We crossed the River Indus at Attock, where Alexander the Great had passed into India many centuries ago.
[pause]
I was met by Major Sir Benjamin Bromhead on my arrival and after a hot bath at my hotel, I was whisked to the Peshawar Club for lunch.

NARRATOR (V.O.)
The Bromheads lived with other officers at Services Hotel. They dined at "Services" Hotel with guests, or at the Peshawar Club, which they called "the Club." Zimmermann and Enders stayed at Dean's Hotel - the most famous hotel in Peshawar. Lord Curzon, Rudyard Kipling, Winston Churchill, and Lowell Thomas had stayed at Dean's. It was torn down a few years ago. Zimmermann wrote to his wife about the first part of their trip after he returned to Peshawar:

ZIMMERMANN
The city of Peshawar is divided into two sections. The cantonment is surrounded by a barbed wire fence with gates on the entrance roads, a protection against the plundering tribes that inhabit this part of the world. The tribes have their own laws with offenses against property taking precedence over lives.

[pause]
On Monday we made a trip into Tribal Territory. Saw the old British fort and walked through the bazaar at Shabkadar. Khassadars – tribal police – were on guard duty, and they lined up to give us a grand reception. The British have fought many battles here, but it's quiet now. We had lunch with the Malik of the lower Mohmand Tribe. We started by having our hands washed by pouring water over them as we sat at the table. There were no implements. Everything was picked up by hand and you weren't supposed to use your left hand. An interesting time. I was a curiosity, being American and in the Navy. We returned for dinner at the Bromheads' hotel, and were joined by Enders, who had arrived from Kabul. On Tuesday, November 16, we began our trip in Enders' jeep, going up the Swat River into the Malakand District. We met the Political Agent, a Major Packman, who showed us the *piquet* – a fort – where the British were holed up, and supposedly Gunga Din came down to get water from the river. Kipling wrote a story about it. We had lunch with the Wali of Swat, a venerable man who is said to have pushed his brother over a cliff. We were greeted by saluting soldiers and a blare of trumpets at the palace gate. The Wali was at the door to welcome us. His palace is outstanding. Persian rugs, modern furniture, up-to-date

plumbing, in the middle of mud huts and buffaloes. Good lunch with many courses. We proceeded on through increasing rugged country, passed the dam and hydroelectric works at the Swat River Canal, and arrived at the home of the P.A. - the Political Agent - to spend the night. Churchill wrote his first book about the Battle of Malakand - it's supposed to be very good. Packman and his wife and two daughters live in the fort with a pet ibex. I think it must be a rather lonely existence. While we were in Malakand, a telegram arrived from Chitral, suggesting that we abandon the trip over Lowari Pass, because it would be too dangerous. The Lowari has never been crossed by a motor vehicle, and it was supposed now to be covered with ice and snow. But Enders decided to make a go of it. The next day, we drove up the road along the Punjkara River to the state of Dir. Our first stop was at Bat Khel to buy rope that would be heavy enough to pull the jeep back on the road, if it might be needed. We then entered the Tribal Territory of Dir State. The *khassadars* wanted to send an escort with us, but Sir Benji said,

              BROMHEAD
Major Enders and Lieutenant Zimmermann are Americans. They are my guests. What would the Americans think if you did not let us pass?

ZIMMERMANN

They opened the gate. [pause] The road to the residence of the Nawab of Dir passed between mountains on which wheat and rice are grown on terraces. We reached Dir in time for tea with the ruler, the Nawab. And with his son, the Waliahad, and their doctor, a captain, in uniform. The bazaar included a *serai* – a caravan resting place – and we saw everything on sale there, from sewing machines to bags of antimony. We left the next morning to make the attempt to cross the pass into Chitral. People thought we were crazy to try to drive over Lowari. The road was really just a donkey caravan trail. We picked up a captain of the Chitral Scouts to act as our guide and translator, and we hired men with donkeys to carry our baggage and to use the rope to pull the jeep, if necessary. We crept along the narrow road with a steep wall on one side and a cliff on the other side, with a river that was hundreds of feet below us. Enders suggested that he drive the jeep alone, and Benji and I and the Scout got out and walked. We arrived for a brief stop at the Gujar Levy Post at 11:00. The road then began to widen so we got back into the jeep to ride to the top of the pass. We reached the summit at 12:30. I was told that it was about 10,000 feet above sea level. The Hindu Kush mountains were directly

in front of us. We were near the
Afghan Border - it was probably
only five miles away, to our left.
A cold, bitter wind was blowing. I
started taking some movies at this
point on the trip. On the north
side of the pass, the road wound
back and forth as it descended into
the state of Chitral. Snow and ice
were ever-present, and there were
trees down which blocked the road.
Benjie and I walked in front of the
jeep to see what was ahead. The
jeep, driven by Enders, slid off of
the road several times, but men
with ropes and donkeys pulled it
back and we finally made it to
Drosh at about 7:30 that evening.
We had gone from 4,000 feet to
10,000, and back to 4,000. It was
quite an exciting trip. We spent
the night and most of the next day
at Drosh. A late departure allowed
the snow and ice to melt on the
north side of the pass. We had
lunch at Drosh on Saturday, and
went on to Chitral, 26 miles away,
arriving at 4:30. The village of
Chitral is surrounded by snow-
capped mountains, the highest being
Tirich Mir - 25,600 feet.

          NARRATOR (V.O.)
The Lowari pass is usually closed
by November 15, so the travelers
were very lucky to have made the
trip successfully. The little
airfield at Drosh, where they
stayed, is a notoriously dangerous
place. The next Mehtar of Chitral
died there in a plane crash. The

summit of Tirich Mir was first reached by a group of Norwegian climbers in 1950. The summit is a bit lower than was estimated in 1943. It is actually 25,230 feet, and it is 24.9 miles from Chiral village. The 1950 climbing party was guided by a young British army officer, Captain Anthony Streather, known as Tony. In the 1960s and 1970s, Tony Streather was one of the most famous mountaineers in the world. He was known for surviving a spectacular fall on K-2 and for his ascents of twenty 20,000-foot mountains in the Himalayas. In 2010, COLONEL ANTHONY STREATHER, OBE, said:

ANTHONY STREATHER

I knew of Sir Benjamin Bromhead, but we never met. He was somewhat of a character. One of the duties of a Political Officer, such as Bromhead, was to be a "bag man" - to bring an impressive tribute to the Mehtar. I hadn't known of this Trip to Chitral. But surely the Trip in 1943 was all part of the Great Game.

ZIMMERMANN

We were fortunate to see the top of Tirich Mir as it is usually in the clouds. But the two days we were there, the weather was perfectly clear, giving us wonderful mountain scenery to look at. We were met by the brother of the Mehtar, with bugles and an honor guard. We went to polo games that were staged for us – this is where polo originated – and then to the Assistant Political Agent's house for drinks. He was the one who sent a telegram, warning us not to attempt to cross the Lowari. We dined at the palace with the Mehtar and several officials who were relatives of his. The state dining and reception room was fantastic, with chandeliers and so forth. We saw Chitral and Hunza dances after dinner – all by men. No women were in evidence in Chitral. In fact, we saw few women anywhere on the trip. We didn't see any sign of Ruskies in Chitral, although migrating Kazaks could be seen at a distance. [pause] The next day, we went horseback riding to watch "hawking," which consists of going to a high place where the river is narrow, getting about 200 men to beat the brush, rousing the birds – *chikhors*, like partridges – to flight, releasing the hawks – falcons – as the *chikhors* fly by, and watching the kill. I drew a spirited ex-polo pony. It took all my strength to hold him down to a slow trot. After lunch we went for a jeep ride about 13 miles north. As soon as we got back the Mehtar had arranged a *markor* shoot. They are mountain deer. Major Enders killed one but didn't have time to see it, as we were leaving for our journey home. It was all very interesting & exciting. I was the first Navy man in Chitral, and there had been only one other

American there before us. The
Mehtar of Chitral and the Nawab of
Dir gave us *chagas* - native coats -
in honor of our visit. We motored
back to Drosh at 5:30, and we
called on the Mehtar's brother. He
is governor of Drosh and heir to
the throne, as the Mehtar has no
legitimate sons. Spent the night
at Drosh Fort mess. [pause] On
Sunday the 21st we had breakfast
and lunch at Drosh and I took
movies of a polo game there. We
left for Ziarat at 2:00 p.m. and
arrived at Ziarat at 4:45 p.m. to
spend the night. We delayed our
departure from Ziarat until 11:00
in the morning of the 22nd to get
sun on the top of the pass. We
spent about 45 minutes on one slick
zig-zag, but the rest of the way up
was comparatively easy. The trip
back down was much the same as
going up. We arrived at Dir at 6
p.m. and spent the night at Dir
rest house on November 22. [pause]

CUT TO:

CAIRO, EGYPT, SHOWING IMAGES OF "SEXTANT," THE FIRST
CAIRO CONFERENCE

          NARRATOR (V.O.)
On November 22, at the same time
that the Three Men were crossing
back over the Lowari Pass to stay
at Dir, President Roosevelt was in
Cairo, where he and Prime Minister
Winston Churchill were planning to
meet to discuss plans for the next
phase of the war. They focused on
the invasion of Europe and made

>   plans for the Pacific theatre.
>   Generalissimo and Madame Chiang
>   Kai-shek were there, too, with a
>   large entourage of his advisors.
>   The conference, code named SEXTANT,
>   would continue until November 26,
>   at which time FDR and Churchill
>   would fly to Tehran to meet with
>   Stalin in the conference known as
>   EUREKA.
>   CUT TO:

ZIRAT, NORTH-WEST FRONTIER PROVINCE, ZIMMERMANN CONTINUES

>   ZIMMERMANN
>   On Tuesday, November 23, we motored
>   160 miles from Dir to Peshawar,
>   with lunch at Malakand. We arrived
>   back pretty well tired out. We
>   will be here for several days.
>   Enders has promised to take me to
>   the Khyber Pass, and on Saturday,
>   the Viceroy of India is visiting
>   Peshawar and we are going to attend
>   the Governor's garden party to meet
>   him. [pause] I signed the
>   Governor's guest book on Wednesday
>   and had dinner with the Bromheads
>   at Services. On Thursday, the
>   25th, I wrote a long letter to
>   Barbara which I hope will pass the
>   censor. Had dinner that evening
>   with the Deputy Commissioner. He
>   is a light-skinned Mohammedan, as
>   are his wife and daughter. We had
>   a delicious dinner and Scotch for a
>   change.
>
>   NARRATOR (V.O.)
>   Zimmermann's handwritten letter
>   would have been difficult for the

censor to read, and it passed without any redactions. Barbara typed a copy of the letter and circulated it to their friends.

CUT TO:

CAIRO, EGYPT, IMAGES CONTINUING OF THE FIRST CAIRO CONFERENCE

> NARRATOR (V.O.) continues
> In Cairo, on Thursday, November 25, President Roosevelt hosted a dinner at the American Embassy in honor of Prime Minister Churchill and Generalissimo and Madame Chiang Kai-shek. It was Thanksgiving, and FDR carved the turkey. [pause] Gordon Enders had vanished after he and Zimmermann and Bromhead arrived back in Peshawar on November 22. He did not reappear until the Governor's garden party for the Viceroy on November 27. Enders was gone for four nights and almost five days. Did he secretly fly a plane to Cairo and return to Peshawar in time to meet the Viceroy? He could probably have gotten a small plane from the U.S. Tenth Air Force base in Peshawar, and he was a skillful pilot. There was plenty of time to make the round trip to Cairo. He would have had little trouble getting through to the V.I.P.s in Cairo, because he was well known to the Chiangs, and also to Louis Dreyfus, who was in Cairo, planning for the Tehran Conference. If Enders did make a secret trip to Cairo, would he have

talked with FDR? And what would he have said? We will probably never know the answer to these questions.

CUT TO:

PESHAWAR, NORTH-WEST FRONTIER PROVINCE, WITH IMAGES OF INDIA

ZIMMERMANN
On Friday evening, I had cocktails and dinner with several friends of the Bromheads. One of them was Mrs. Dorothy Leeper - her husband, Colonel William Leeper, is the Home Secretary of the province. I first met her when I passed through Peshawar the first time. The next day, Benjie took me up to the Khyber Pass. We entered Tribal Territory at Jamrud, about 9 miles from Pesahwar. A rail line went beside the winding road for about 32 miles to Landi Khana, but it ended before the road crossed into Afghanistan. Many blockhouses and tank traps were along the road, and I saw forts at Shagai and Landi Khotal. Benjie pointed out that the Afridis were on either side of the road as far as Landi Khotal, and Mullagaris were a short distance to the north. The Shingari Tribe are then along the rest of the way to the pass and on the other side of it as it goes down into Afghanistan.

BROMHEAD
In 1930 Peshawar was threatened by an Afridi Lushkar, which surrounded the city. And since 1937, the Axis

has caused unrest among the Afridis, and in 1938, parts of the Afridi tribe stared a march on Jalalabad to loot it and embarrass the Afghan government. They were stopped by a blockade and made to pay a penalty in guns.

                ZIMMERMANN
Benjie told me that a Sikh general was killed in battle at the Khyber about 200 years ago. Believing this would sway the hopes of the enemy, they pickled his body and stuck it in one of the windows of the fort at Jamrud, where they could periodically show it to the enemy. On the way back, we had tea with a Subhardar Major and his son. Both were decorated for valor. That afternoon, the Governor of the North-West Frontier Province had a garden party to meet the Viceroy. Major Bromhead arranged for Enders and me to be invited. It was a grand affair in a beautiful setting on the Government House lawn. All the Maliks from the surrounding country were there along with important Britishers of the community. The Viceroy had heard we'd been up the Lowari to Chitral in a jeep, so he came over to where we were standing and asked all about it. Enders did the talking as he has a flare for it and modesty is not one of his virtues.

                NARRATOR (V.O.)
Enders doubtless reminded Wavell that they had met two years earlier

in Delhi, when he was their guest at dinner. He would have mentioned Lady Wavell and their beautiful daughters. Wavell would have been especially interested in the jeep ride over the Lowari, because as a young man, riding on horseback behind a senior officer, he watched in horror as the other officer's horse bolted. Horse and rider fell off the road, out of sight. To Wavell's amazement, they fell into some bushes and survived. They were hauled back onto the road with only scrapes and bruises. [pause] Zimmermann's comment about Enders is reflective of what others, unknown to Zimmermann, also said about Enders. ALGHAN LUSEY, an O.S.S. officer, who knew Enders in China before the war, wrote to William Donovan, saying that

ALGHAN LUSEY
Enders is a bag of wind. I recommend replacing him.

NARRATOR
It is not clear what Lusey meant, because Enders was never in Donovan's chain of command. But his comment shows that Enders could inspire others to speak ill of him. For instance, when asked about Enders in 2010, Minister Cornelius Engert's son RODERICK ENGERT - who as young man in Afghanistan knew Enders well - said:

RODERICK ENGERT
Enders - he was a blowhard.

NARRATOR (V.O.)
As a teen-ager, Roderick Engert left his family in Afghanistan and went to India to work for the O.S.S. as a translator. After the war, he went to Yale and had a career in government service.

ZIMMERMANN
After the garden party I went to a dance at the Club. I listened to fox trots, waltzes and a tango, but my heart wasn't in it. I didn't dance. [pause] The next day, November 28, I finished writing up my notes, had lunch at the Club with the Bromheads, and went to a gun factory in the afternoon - took some movies there and had tea with a major and his son. Back to Peshawar for dinner at the Commissioner's.

CUT TO:

TEHRAN, IRAN, WITH IMAGES OF THE TEHRAN CONFERENCE OF FDR, CHURCHILL, AND STALIN, AT THE EMBASSY OF THE U.S.S.R.

NARRATOR (V.O.)
At the same time that Zimmermann and Bromhead were visiting a gun factory near Peshawar, FDR and Churchill met Stalin for the first time in Iran. It was November 28, 1943. This was Stalin's first trip, and probably his only trip, outside of the Soviet Union. The conference was code named EUREKA. The conference was organized by the

U.S. Minister to Iran, Louis Goethe Dreyfus, who was Gordon Enders' mentor in the State Department. After the war, Dreyfus was appointed as the U.S. Ambassador to Afghanistan. The Tehran Conference was held at the Soviet Embassy, because of rumors of a possible attack by German commandos. The "Big Three" - FDR, Churchill, and Stalin - agreed that the invasion of France - Operation OVERLORD - would take place by May 1944. D-Day was actually a month later, on June 6. And they agreed on the independence of Iran. Patrick Hurley, now a major general, was there as an advisor to FDR. He was one of the last to leave Tehran. Hurley then visited several other cities in Iran before leaving on his own plane for India on December 21. He would arrive in Afghanistan in January 1944. Enders, who was then in Delhi, flew back to Kabul.

CUT TO:

NORTH-WEST FRONTIER PROVINCE, WITH IMAGES OF THE TRIP

ZIMMERMANN
We left Peshawar for the long trip to Quetta at 8:00 a.m. on Monday morning, the 29th. It was the 18th day since I left Karachi. We entered Waziristan, in Tribal Territory, and reached Kohat at 9:35, a trip of 41.9 miles.

NARRATOR (V.O.)
Zimmermann didn't say it, but this part of the trip was especially

dangerous. Only one American previously traveled across the tribal territory of Waziristan between Quetta and Peshawar. It was in 1926, and Lowell Thomas made the trip in the other direction, from Quetta to Peshawar. He was also probably the first non-governmental American citizen to cross the Khyber Pass. Lowell Thomas spent a night at the home of a British officer in North Waziristan. The next day, after he left, the officer's wife and daughter were kidnapped. The daughter was eventually rescued, but her mother was killed. By chance, Zimmermann met that officer thirteen years later, as he rode on the train from Karachi to Peshawar. And he probably saw him again in Swat, at Nowshera, on the road to Mingora - where the travelers met the Wali at his palace.

ZIMMERMANN

We left Kohat at 10:55 and reached Thal at 1:15 - 104 miles. We had tiffin - tea - there, and then went on to Parchinar at 3:42, 160.3 miles, and arrived at 6:15 p.m. We had breakfast the next morning at Kohat with the Political Agent, Sheikh Sahib, and his brother, Mir Ali, the District Commissioner. The D.C.'s house was beautiful, with terraced gardens and palm trees. We lunched at the Station Mess in Thal with Brigadier Barstow. He sent armored carriers to watch over us for 10 miles out of Thal. We had tea and dined at Parchinar with the P.A. for Kurram, Kenneth Donald, and several other British and Indian officers and their wives. The next day, we went to the Afghan border with Kenneth Donald, a Lieutenant-Colonel Francis, Sir Benjamin, and about 15 rifles of the Kurram Militia. To get there, we drove about 15 miles from Parichanar, and then hiked up to Peiwar Khotal. It is a 10,000-foot broad mountain pass on the border. We lunched on top of One Gun Hill, which was the scene of an engagement between Afghans and Lord Roberts in 1879. It was also involved in the Third Afghan War in 1919. An Afghan outpost was in sight at our altitude just over the border, and behind it was a range of high mountains. Sir Benjie said about this place:

BROMHEAD
Peiwar Khotal is potentially the most powerful position in the world.

NARRATOR (V.O.)
The Peiwar Khotal pass that Bromhead described as "potentially the most powerful position in the world" is on the border of Afghanistan. It is near the mountains on the Afghan side which contain the Tora Bora Caves. Bromhead's comment was eerily prescient. These caves are where Osama bin-Laden hid successfully from the American troops that were

sent to find him after the 9/11 attack in 2001. Colonel Anthony Streather, who guided the first ascent of Tirich Mir, recalled having been there when he was stationed in Pakistan in the late 1940s. Streather received the M.B.E. for his work as a peace-keeper in Cyprus. His M.B.E. was superseded by the O.B.E. for climbing. In 2010, Tony Streather recalled his time in the North-West Frontier Province:

STREATHER

I was born in 1926 in England and was educated there. I went to India after the war and was commissioned in the Indian Army. I arrived in Chitral in about 1949 or '50, shortly before the Norwegian team arrived to climb Tirich Mir. I never heard about the trip that was taken in 1943, and I didn't know any of the people who were involved, although I heard about Bromhead many times. Yes, the trip in 1943 - it was all part of the Great Game. The Russians had come into Chitral previously, and they got interested in this area again a bit later, sometime after 1943. And yes, Peiwar Khotal and the Kurram Valley are close to Tora Bora. Osama Bin Laden hid there after 9/11. I have been in one of the Tora Bora caves.

ZIMMERMANN

From Peiwar, we motored to Karlachi on the Afghan border at the point where the Kurram River flows into India. Peiwar and Karlachi are the two main routes from Afghanistan in these parts. We had tea at the militia post at the foot of Peiwar and returned to Parichinar for drinks and dinner at the Kurram Militia Mess. Parachinar is at an altitude of about 3,800 feet. [pause] On Wednesday, December 1, we left Parchinar at 9:40 and arrived at Thal at 11:35, 54 miles, in about two hours. Here we picked up a Wazir Tribal Escort and proceeded to Spinwam, and then to the nearby town of Miram Shah where we spent the night. The country around Thal is heavily filled with tank traps as defense against the threat of a possible German attack in July 1942. [pause] We were met by Major Denning and then went to Mir Ali, where we met Lt.-Col. Janson and he accompanied us to Miram Shah. We arrived there at 2:55 p.m. We stayed at the Tochi Scouts Mess. The Tochi Valley is occupied by Daurs. They are Sunnis, who asked for British protection. However, Daurs are considered a bad lot, having conspired with the Faqir of Ipi, whose village is on the Tochi River near here. Ipi is now on the Afghan border, northwest of Miram Shah. Two of his guns were reported moving on camels past Dosali, which is near here.

NARRATOR (V.O.)
The Faqir of Ipi was the most successful of all of the tribal

leaders who led rebellions in the 20th century against governments on both sides of the Border. He operated from well-hidden bases in both Afghanistan and British India. He was never captured, and never conquered. Not by the British and its militias along the Border. And after Independence, the Pakistan military also failed to defeat him. He was a Pathan, which was the majority tribe on both sides of the Border, and he convinced his followers that he was a leader with both spiritual power - a mullah - and temporal power - a malik. This combination gave him great authority. In the nineteenth and twentieth centuries, Britain had been bedeviled by a succession of tribal leaders who claimed to be both malik and mullah. In the present century, Mullah Omar, who led the Taliban to great success, followed the same pattern: a man who claimed to be both mullah and malik. The U.S. Minister to Afghanistan, CORNELIUS ENGERT, wrote several messages to the State Department in 1943 and 1944 which told of Ipi as a dangerous man.

CORNELIUS ENGERT
There are many bands of brigands operating in the south of Afghanistan. Their robberies and depredations have caused many deaths. The Border is a very dangerous place. The principal rebel leader in the Faqir of Ipi. Next to him in importance are

Abdurrahaman, known as "Pak," and in the south, in addition to Ipi and Pak, is Mazrak Khan, known as "Mazrak."

ZIMMERMANN

2,000 rupees is ordinary blood money for a murder in this part of the world, and once accepted, it settles the murder. A murder can be bought for 50-100 rupees, which is less than the cost of a rifle. At Miram Shah, we heard that 10 Hindu women were kidnapped and taken into Afghanistan; also, that a Hindu shopkeeper was kidnapped, probably on information from his Hindu competitor. Ransom was demanded for the shopkeeper - 7,000 rupees - with negotiations underway. The girls aren't considered worth ransoming. [pause] Since we've been here, a road engineer's lorry was held up, and the supervisor was being held for ransom. Another lorry was held up and three of the highwaymen were killed, one an Afghan. The R.A.F. bombed some outlaws who were hiding in caves, to good effect. There's huge airdrome at Miram Shah near the Tochi Scout outpost at Spinwam. Such is life on the Northwest Frontier. It costs millions every year to keep it in as good order as it is at present. [pause] On Tuesday, December 2, we left Miram Shah after breakfast. We passed back through Dosali and went on to Iblanke Post. We arrived back at Dosali at 1 o'clock, and had a big *tikala* – dinner – and we spent the night there. It had been a hectic day. We saw a brigadier who had just come from Razmak, on the border. He was shot up while he was out with his brigade on a practice maneuver. Tochi Scouts escorted us to Dosali. Along the way, we went past a 5.5 inch gun and truck which had fallen over, killing two and wounding a dozen more of the militia men. While we were in Dosali, about twenty shots were fired from a hill into the Army camp about a half mile from us. Fortunately, no one was hurt. [pause] Benjie was in this part of Waziristan for the past several years as commander of the Zhob militia. He told me about the situation in the various tribes.

BROMHEAD

All of the tribes above the Kabul River – north of Peshawar – are quiet and easy to handle. The tribes are left alone. They are ruled by Maliks, who cooperate with the Wali of Swat, the Nawab of Dir, and the Mehtar of Chitral. However, south of Pesahawar, the Wazirs and Mahsuds take democracy to the point of anarchy. They will not listen to Maliks or Khans unless it suits them and they are difficult to handle. The tribes in the Zhob area are democratic and willing to heed their Maliks and are not a great problem.

ZIMMERMANN

On Friday, December 3, we left Dosali at 10:15 in the morning and reached Miram Shah at 11:25. Went back to stay with the Lowis. He had received word that an Indian Army Engineer lorry had been held up near Datta Kheyl, a supervisor kidnapped and two men wounded. A dicker for the kidnapped man's release was reported for 7,000 rupees. Two 500-pound bombs were dropped on a gang of tribesmen who lived in caves near Miram Shah. Later reports said no casualties, but good moral results. Grazing grounds are the keys to tribal behavior. Benjie told me that:

BROMHEAD

The job of controlling the tribes is not a military one, but the Scouts must do it. They are the local militia, but they are from other areas. For deserters, a system of amnesties might be useful, if it works.

ZIMMERMANN

December 4 was a long day on the road. We left Miram Shah at 9:30 a.m. and had a big tea at Mir Ali at 11:00. We picked up Major Denning to take him to Bannu. It is prosperous, compared to towns in the Tribal Territories. The land is rich. We passed large groups of Gilzais migrating from Afghanistan for the winter. Benjie says:

BROMHEAD
Generally speaking, the whole Gilzai Tribe are friendly to the British. However, one small subdivision, known as the Dinar Kheyl - some 50 families - are sneak thieves and make trouble in the area between Tannai and Gul Kutch.

ZIMMERMANN
We arrived at Tank at 2:30 p.m. We took the Acting Political Agent, "Pat" Duncan, in our jeep from Tank to Jandola. We were accompanied by an armored truck with our baggage and *khaddasar* guards. We arrived at Jandola at 3:45 p.m. Jandola is the headquarters of the South Waziristan Scouts, who are commanded by a Colonel Janson. The P.A. - Duncan - and his wife have a large 1-story bungalow. On three sides, it surrounds a courtyard. The yard is barren and it is quite cold here at this time of year. [pause] The next morning - Sunday, was my 24th day away from Karachi - we left Jandola for Wana after breakfast. I traveled with Benjie in a Mahsud lorry, escorted by an armored lorry that was provided by Duncan. It was bristling with *khaddasars*, rifles up and on the ready. Enders and his sergeant - Tommy Nicholson - rode in the middle of our little caravan in his jeep. We had morning tea at Sora Rogha with Kushwakht, a brother of the Mehtar of Chitral, and we lunched at Ladha. A tower there

was recently hit by a 4.5 inch gun because its owner refused to turn over a murderer who had killed on post property. We had afternoon tea at Tiarze and passed through Koniguram to arrive at Wana at 7:20 p.m. Benjie told us about the Mahsuds:

BROMHEAD

Koniguram is the capital town of all three Mahsud tribes. In it live Uramurs, who speak no known language. They are artisans, making knives and guns, and some now take to lorry driving. The Uramurs feed jirga members without charge when they visit Kaniguram. Jirgas are meetings of tribal elders who come together to settle disputes, and the host provides the hospitality. It's their protection fee. The census shows some 100,000 Mahsuds but Duncan believes they are 150,000 with about 20,000 rifles. He reported that a lorry was shot up in Mahsud territory with an Afghan Malik killed. The border is very porous here. Janson estimates that Wazirs have more than the 30,000 rifles that they have declared.

NARRATOR (V.O.)

Zimmermann began a new letter to his wife on Monday, December 6. He added to it on the 9th and ended it on the 15th, after he had returned to Karachi. He wrote from Wana:

                    ZIMMERMANN
This will have to be in pencil as
my fountain pen has run dry and
there's no sign of any ink in this
place. It's been over a week since
I've written to you. I just
haven't had time. We've been on
the go ever since. We decided to
rest up today as we are pretty worn
out. We're at Wana, which is
occupied by a brigade of the
British and Indian Army. It's
about 10 miles from the Afghanistan
border. The one-story buildings are
on level land, and there are low
hills in the background. No
vegetation in sight. Pretty bleak.
We will spend the night here.

                                            CUT TO:

CAIRO, EGYPT, THE AMERICAN EMBASSY.

                    NARRATOR (V.O.)
Before they left Tehran on December
1, FDR and Churchill agreed to
return to Cairo to meet with
President Ismet Inonu of Turkey, to
discuss the possibility that Turkey
might join the Allies. In the end,
it was agreed only that Turkey
would remain neutral. Churchill
was becoming ill and he nearly died
of pneumonia as he flew home across
North Africa. General Patrick
Hurley flew to several cities in
Iran at the time of the Second
Cairo Conference, and he sent a
report of his observations to FDR
on December 21. He then flew to
other areas in Asia, and in January
1944, he piloted his own plane to

India and Ceylon, where he met Lord Mountbatten.

ZIMMERMANN

On Tuesday, December 7, we left Wana at 9:00 a.m. and reached Tanai, ten miles away, at 10:30. Met Enders there in his jeep, and left at 10:55 and crossed into Baluchistan at Gul Kutch at noon – 26 miles in an hour. Slow going. At Gul Kutch, we were met by Major Peter Garret, commander of the Zhob militia. Garett knew Bromhead, who was his predecessor as the commander of the Zhob Militia. We left Gul Kutch at 12:45 and arrived at Sambaza at 1:30 for lunch. We left Sambaza at 3:00 and reached the *piquet* of Tora Gharu in a half-hour, at the top of a rugged hill. I was told that it's relatively peaceful at Sambaza, and no escorts would be needed. We spent an hour there and then drove on to arrive at Fort Sandeman at 5:15. It is the headquarters of the Zhob Militia. The total mileage today was 79 – very slow going. We dined at the Zhob Militia Mess with the P.A., a man named Searle, and his wife, and a Brigadier Purvis. The Searles live in the fort, but they take to the hills behind it in the summer. I roomed with Major Garrett and Enders' sergeant. Garrett was in civilian clothing, but he was very much the military man and was properly saluted everywhere we went. The market place beside the fort was interesting. I took a picture of camels that were lined up for a long drink at the trough there. And of a man in a head dress, looking at me, impassively. I wondered what he was thinking.

NARRATOR (V.O.)
Zimmermann thought he would finally have a day of rest, but he was mistaken. Instead, the three Anglo-American officers went on a long trip with armed escorts. They reached the Afghan border again.

ZIMMERMANN
On December 8, my 27th day on this trip, we went in Colonel Keating's car with two escort trucks and an engineer's station wagon to see a new road being made to Shawet. It's on the border. It is the big entry route for Gilzais, the Suleimen Kheyl, the Nazras, and other tribes. We visited Fort Shahigu, altitude 6695 ft., and traveled along an old road across the plain for 7 miles and then a new road to a work camp for 14 miles; and then for another five miles for lunch at the border. We left Sandeman at 10:00 a.m. and were back at 8:00 p.m., having traveled 156 miles. [pause] Water is sometimes scarce in Sandeman. I was told that wells had to be sunk as deep as 80 feet, because not enough water comes down from the mountains. [pause] On the road today, we saw a crowd off of the road. Thought there was trouble but it turned out to be a

cremation. A Hindu Army recruit had been killed and his friends had built a bonfire and were disposing of his remains. [pause] We also passed by a Hindubagh Gulzai camp. The Gulzai tribes wander across the border from Afganistan. Their Afghan dress is more colorful than that of the Indian. Their horses are handsome, and they are good riders. The horses are protected from the cold weather by heavy woven blankets that are strapped around them. Benjie tells me that the Gulzais are famous for locating underground streams. I took some pictures of them. [pause] Tomorrow we leave for Quetta, and after that, I'll return to Karachi. I'll be glad to get back. While it's been very interesting, it's also be very hectic. None of these places have modern plumbing. I'm tired of bathing in a wash tub and washing in a basin. Also, it's been quite cold, because of the altitude - between 4 and 10,000 feet. Not so bad here - only 4,500. My place in Enders' jeep is in the back seat. It's open, of course, and the breezes and dust make life far from comfortable, especially in the back seat. I finally picked up a cold, one of the good ones. [pause] Most of this country is pretty God-forsaken. You marvel that anyone can scratch a living out if it. That's partly the trouble. Some can't, so they take to plunder and pillaging. [pause] We motored to Quetta on Thursday, the 9th. We left Sandeman at 9:10 and arrived at the Residency at 5:05 p.m. We had tea at the Zhob Militia Post outside of Hindu Bagh, where large encampments of Karotis live. They are Gilzais who make a trade out of digging for karez, an ore of chromium. Benjie says:

BROMHEAD
The chrome mines here produce 40,000 tons annually of 52% ore, which is exported to the U.S. A man named "Pop" Wynn runs the mines. He employs some 6,000 camels and donkeys to carry ore down from the mountains, and he has a one-meter gauge spur track and some lend lease trucks.

ZIMMERMANN
We passed a shepherd and his "fat-tailed" sheep near Quetta. The tail is said to be a great delicacy, and their wool makes the finest carpets. I took some photos of the shepherd and a close-up of one of the sheep. We might want to find a broker in Quetta to do business with after the war. Who knows? [pause] We stayed at the "residency" which consists of tents – very elaborate, however. It is near the Temporary Government House in Quetta. The old Government House was destroyed in an earthquake in 1935, and the His Excellency, the Governor, Lieutenant-Colonel William Hay, lives with his family in temporary quarters while a new Government

House is being built. In 1935, Quetta was the scene of one of the earth's worst quakes. 30,000 people were killed out a population of 120,000. Practically the whole town was levelled. His Excellency and his family live in tin shacks. You'd be surprised to see how comfortable they've made the tents of the "residency" and the tin shacks of the governor's quarters. [pause]

On Friday, I saw Major-General Money and Colonel Bruce-Steer of Baluchistan H.Q. And also "Father" Wood - not a priest, that's just his nickname - and two British majors. And I rested. [pause]

We were royally entertained by His Excellency. On Saturday, Enders and Benjie and I went for the day beyond the Hannah Valley for a *chikhor* shoot with Governor and Mrs. Hays and their children, and Major Woods-Ballard, Political Agent for Quetta. I tried to take movies and pictures with my borrowed camera of the interesting scenes - I hope they turn out all right. We saw a donkey laden with our lunch, which was cooked beside an open fire - roasted mutton on stakes. The beaters for the *chikhor* shoot sat in a circle to one side, and they knelt to say their noon-day prayers. We sat on a large tarp that was secured at the corners to keep it from blowing away. We all dressed very warmly, of course. Enders was in his usual sheepskin bomber jacket with the collar turned up and his aviator's cap pulled down close to his ears. He didn't have his pistol and ammunition belt on for a change. The governor had on a coat that reached to the ground. The delightful Hays children sat with us. The governor had a dinner party for us in the evening.

NARRATOR (V.O.)
Zimmermann continued his letter to his wife, Barbara, after he got back to Karachi.

ZIMMERMANN
We left the next day, Sunday, December 12. I left on the train for Karachi. Major Alston, Mrs. Wood, Benjie, Enders, and Sergeant Tommy were at the station to see me off. Enders and Tommy planned to drive his jeep back to Kabul, passing directly from Quetta into Afghanistan. And Benjie would go as soon as he could arrange for an armored escort to go back to Peshawar. [pause] The train passed through about a dozen tunnels as it went through Baluchistan and into the Sind province. It took two days to go on the dusty train ride from Quetta to Karachi, and I was glad to be "home" again. Five letters from you and one from Warren awaited me, adding greatly to the joy of being back, "be it ever so humble." Karachi isn't a bad place at all after one has seen other parts of India.

NARRATOR (V.O.)
Zimmermann's orders to "Proceed to Peshawar" were endorsed to show that he returned to duty at Naval Liaison Office Karachi at 1130 on Wednesday, 15 December 1943, 34 days after he had left Karachi. He wrote to his wife on December 28,

ZIMMERMANN
I'm afraid my last letters have been awfully dull, concentrating on my trip and telling you how much I was missing you and how anxious I am to be back again with you. [pause] I finally got rid of the worst of my cold, but I still cough – mostly at night, which rather disturbs my slumbers. Day before yesterday Charles Thayer came to see me. He is now on his way to London to be on some mission there. He has had some very interesting experiences. He's coming for dinner tomorrow night and leaving the next day. He brought a letter from Enders, enclosing a length of cloth from Chitral. I am sending it to you, along with some things for the children that I brought back from the trip along the north-west frontier.

ENDERS
Here is the length of Chitrali *putthu* which I promised you. Luckily for me Thayer is able to bring it to you by hand due to his sudden transfer to London. Thayer's transfer was not the only surprise I got on my return. I'm

leaving day after tomorrow for New Delhi. Tommy and I got out of Quetta on schedule and made our trip back as planned without a hitch. We did the run from Khandahar to Kabul in one day. Surprisingly, we encountered no snow on the road, nor rain, nor anything else disagreeable. I'd be glad to hear how the movies turned out and whether or not I will be able to get prints.

           NARRATOR (V.O.)
Zimmermann's movies were sent back to the U.S. to be developed, and they were reviewed by a Navy censor before they were forwarded to his wife. She didn't receive all of the ones that he wrote home about. Some were probably lost in transit, and some may have been destroyed by the censor. Zimmermann never saw any of them until he returned to the U.S. Enders never received any of them. [pause] On January 2, Zimmermann was sent to Colombo, Ceylon, on a courier mission. He was probably debriefed at that time at the U.S. Naval Headquarters about his trip along the Border of Afghanistan. He returned via Bombay and was back in Karachi on January 6th. [pause]
As Zimmermann was flying back from Ceylon, Enders was preparing to return to Kabul. He learned that FDR's special representative, Major General Patrick Hurley, had received permission from the Afghans to fly into the country in

his personal military airplane. He was allowed to be in uniform, accompanied by nine U.S. military officers and a supporting staff of enlisted personnel. The Afghans were looking forward to this visit, because they hoped the U.S. would serve as a foil against other governments which they considered to be dangerous - especially the Russians and British. Hurley had flown to Karachi, then New Delhi, and finally Peshawar, where he arrived on January 3. Bad weather and problems with his aircraft delayed his departure. Hurley and his party finally departed in automobiles from Peshawar on January 8. Enders had wired Cornelius Engert on January 7, saying that he was returning the next day to Kabul. Hurley, now in Kabul, asked Mountbatten to send him a C-47, and Enders probably hitched a ride on this plane to Kabul instead of driving. The C-47, possibly with Enders on board, arrived on January 12. Enders had prepared a 5-page brief about Afghanistan, which he presented to Hurley on the 13th. The paper does not mention Enders' trip with Zimmermann and Bromhead along the border of India. The unique, first-ever trip that was completed less than a month earlier was probably something that Enders would mention verbally to Hurley. Hurley and his entire party, including Enders, flew out of Afghanistan the next day on

Mountbatten's C-47. After a brief stop in Peshawar, they flew on to New Delhi. Enders then typed up a 5-page report to summarize the impressions that Hurley had made on the Afghans. Both reports were preserved and are in the Hurley archives at the University of Oklahoma. The key points of Enders' status report to General Hurley are followed by his comments about the general's visit.

ENDERS

Afghan rule is very weak and exists merely because the ruling clan is able to keep the various factions in the country divided amongst themselves. This is to say that Afghanistan is not a homogenous nation but instead it is a conglomeration of Pathan tribes along its eastern and southern frontiers; Tajiks, Uzbeks and Arabs along its northern and western frontiers; and Mongoloid Hazaras in the central mountainous districts directly west of Kabul. [pause] The upshot of Afghan fear of Russia and mistrust of Great Britain has been the development of several crippling handicaps for Afghanistan. She has bowed to the wishes of both Russia and Great Britain in keeping the country backward and unimproved. The Afghans say that Russia believes that "Afghanistan is the road to India." The United States will no doubt enjoy a most favored position for the purpose of rehabilitating

the Afghan military establishment and supplying the government of Afghanistan with rapid means of communications such as radio, telephone, telegraph and all-weather highways. But if such a program for Afghanistan is undertaken by America there will be considerable obstruction encountered from both Russia and Great Britain. [pause]
The favorable impact of General Hurley's visit to Kabul was very marked. While Turkey, Iran, Iraq, Egypt, etc., had either shared or participated in the Teheran conference, Afghanistan had been left out entirely. The Afghans were eager for some notice from the United States, although they remained too proud to invite it. General Hurley's visit afforded Afghanistan a direct channel to the United States, which are now looked to as the arbiter of Afghan-Russian and Afghan-British relations.

NARRATOR (V.O.)
Betty Enders was never one to miss an opportunity, and in April 1944, she used Hurley's visit as a gateway to FDR. She wrote to Hurley:

BETTY ENDERS
Dear General Hurley, During your recent visit to Afghanistan, my husband, who was then our Military Attaché, wrote me much of your friendly and considerate treatment of him. He also sent me pictures

of you and your plane and crew, which you may realize were of great interest to me. Some time ago, Gordon sent me some Afghan stamps to do with as I liked. As I am not a collector, I have given away the greater number of them, but I have thirteen of them left. It has occurred to me that if President Roosevelt does not have any of these in his collection, I should be glad to give them to him. Knowing that you were there as his personal representative, I felt that the best way to offer them was through you. Gordon has been sent to New Delhi with the status of Military Observer, but I think he is already homesick for Kabul. My husband greatly enjoyed your visit to Kabul, and I hope that someday I may have the pleasure of meeting you. Sincerely yours, Elizabeth C. Enders

NARRATOR (V.O.)
In the meantime, on January 7, Secretary of State Hull wired Minister Engert, saying that Captain Ernest Fox had been transferred from Alaska as relief for Major Enders, pending approval by Engert. Fox was an oil and mineral geologist. He had a record of exploration in Afghanistan before World War II. Engert said Yes, and Fox was appointed as Enders' successor. Fox traveled first to Delhi, where he met Enders. From Delhi, the two officers traveled together to

Peshawar, and then on to Kabul. Enders spent more than two weeks in Kabul, orienting Fox. He then returned to Delhi, intending to continue as an intelligence officer - a "Military Observer" - in the India-Ceylon Theatre. Enders had a good relationship with two other key U.S. intelligence agencies in India - the very secretive Joint Intelligence Collection Agency (JICA), and Naval Intelligence. His relationship with the third agency - the O.S.S. - may have been somewhat fraught. We heard earlier that Alghan Lusey, an O.S.S. agent in China, called him a "bag of wind." But the head of the O.S.S. mission in India was Colonel Suydam Cutting, who - like Enders - had a strong personal connection with Tibet. They would probably have gotten along well. Nevertheless, Enders did not finish the war in India. He contracted a serious case of malaria and was sent back to the U.S. in March 1944. [pause] Zimmermann had written to Bromhead when he returned to Karachi on January 6, after having being debriefed in Ceylon. Benjie replied on the 15th.

BROMHEAD
Dear Al, Thank you so much for your letter, which I should have answered sooner. It was good of you to write when you were suffering from that cold - It seemed a really bad one when I left you in the train, and I was glad to

hear that you were getting over it. I found it rather hard to do all I should do in recent weeks, as Nancy suddenly produced her baby, a son, in the early hours of the 21st December, and on account of complications has only just left hospital – so all my spare time has been spent in visiting her. She was terribly distressed at first as the boy was born with a cleft palate and hare lip – it was a sad anti-climax for her – but she has now recovered, as she realizes that the matter can be put right by a good surgeon. It's beginning to look as if we shall have to send the child to England, as after three weeks of writing and writing we have had no news of any plastic surgeon out here. We had a rather quiet Christmas and New Year owing to Nancy being in hospital – but she herself is now alright and the boy seems to be doing well. I enjoyed our tour together and it was nice of you to be so appreciative. I've not heard or seen anything of Gordon since Quetta, but I believe he's been down to Delhi recently, as I met Tommy the other day. I've not had the films from Bombay yet, I hope they've not lost them. [pause] Well Al, I hope you've quite recovered from the cold and are fit. I'm off to Delhi on the 3rd or 4th of February. Nancy joins me in sending our best wishes and good luck for 1944. Yours aye, Benjie.

NARRATOR (V.O.)
Zimmermann wrote to his wife on March 4, saying that his nephew, a captain in the U.S. Army Ordnance Corps, had recently seen Enders in Delhi. He asked her about writing an account of the trip for a civilian magazine:

ZIMMERMANN
Should I write up the trip through the North-West Frontier Province? I don't think the Navy wants it. I don't think it will be good enough to be published, so I hate to put in the time. But if you really think there's a hope, I'll go ahead with it.

NARRATOR (V.O.)
We don't know what Barbara said in reply, but she must have encouraged him. The next month Zimmermann wrote again about this:

ZIMMERMANN
I will continue to write up my North-West Frontier Province trip but I'm afraid it's going to take a long time for me to finish it. There just isn't spare time, and letter writing takes up most of what there is.

NARRATOR (V.O.)
Zimmermann never finished writing an article about the Trip for a magazine. But in April, he heard good news from Lady NANCY BROMHEAD, who wrote:

LADY NANCY BROMHEAD
You will be glad to know that John Desmond is now out of hospital; I wish I could see him before he goes home. I am busy with the other two, & weary! Anne has just had sand fly fever. Ben has been to Delhi lately, then was here about 3 days & is now in Dera Ismail Khan until Monday. I shall have to wait for him to get your address. I hope you have good news from home. Yours sincerely, Nancy Bromhead

NARRATOR (V.O.)
By June 1944, but probably much earlier, in the small world of the British ex-patriates in India in the time of the Raj, Zimmermann learned that two of his bridge partners in Karachi were well acquainted with Sir Benjamin and Lady Nancy Bromhead. Lady Vere Birdwood, who later became the Countess Birdwood, was the daughter-in-law of Sir Benjie's aunt; and her husband, Christopher Birdwood, who was heir to an Earldom, was in the Waziristan Campaign with Bromhead in 1919-1920. And Colonel Geoffrey and April Swayne-Thomas had been good friends of Benjie before the war in Quetta. Benjie mentioned her in a letter to Zimmermann on April 4. [pause] Early in June, Gene Markey passed through Karachi:

ZIMMERMANN
Dearest Barb, [pause] Captain Gene Markey passed through here several

days ago. He's been down to Ceylon
and is on his way home for a visit.
I wish I could do that.

          NARRATOR (V.O.)
On his trip home, Markey left India
forever. Curt Winsor wrote to
Zimmermann in July from Washington:

          WINSOR
Markey is not returning to India
and his successor has not been
named, so I don't know who will
determine courier trips home in his
absence.

          NARRATOR (V.O.)
And on July 26, Zimmermann wrote
about Enders once again:

          ZIMMERMANN
Gordon Enders has evidently written
an article on Afghanistan for the
Saturday Evening Post. I haven't
seen it yet. I imagine it is one
of the May issues or perhaps early
June. When I see it I'll give you
the exact issue. Perhaps he'll
write one about our trip thru the
North-West Frontier Province, maybe
use my pictures. I kind of
suspected he would, that is why
I've never been too enthusiastic
about doing it myself. I thought
by the time I got around to it he
would have an article already
published. Besides that's what he
normally lives on anyway. He is
now back in the states, having
contracted a bad dose of malaria.

NARRATOR (V.O.)
Zimmermann mentioned Enders only once more in his letters from India, and he never spoke about Enders to his children. No article by Enders appeared in the *Saturday Evening Post*, although five years after the war was over, Enders published a prize-winning story in *Collier's* magazine, based on his experiences in Afghanistan. Nothing was ever published by any of the three travelers about the trip they took along the frontier.
[pause]
On September 5, 1944, Zimmermann wrote a letter to his wife in which he gave his most complete explanation of the purpose of the trip, to the extent that the censors would allow:

ZIMMERMANN
Now, as regards to the pictures. You are very nice to be so enthusiastic and to go to all that trouble in peddling them. I'm afraid your enthusiasm is biased by the fact your boy took them. Probably by now you will have found they are unacceptable anyway, which would settle the matter. But if there is a glimmer of hope still left, there could be something done about it. I'm not awfully proud of the North-West Frontier ones. I had to take about 50 pictures with a strange camera using filters before I ever saw the results of my work. Then, they are contact prints done by photographic shops

along the way. With the negatives in hand I'm sure experts could do more with them in enlarging.
[pause] As to why I was there: It was a very nice gesture on the part of British Intelligence (with whom we have the finest cooperation) to invite one of our officers to make the trip that had already been instigated by the Military Attaché to Kabul - Major Enders - to give him an opportunity to see what was on the other side of the fence. Then again, I think the British are anxious to let her ally have a look at some of her problems in India, to counteract the crack pots who came over here and after six weeks write a book about the oppression of the Indian people, and how they should unquestionably have their independence. Anyway, I took the trip and took the pictures and there are very few people - and I might say only two Americans - that have ever taken such a comprehensive trip of the Tribal Territory. As far as peddling them to a magazine is concerned, I'm sure I should have Sir Benjamin's permission and also the Navy Department. I've written them both today - just in case. As far as a story goes - I started one some time ago - a bit more in detail than anything I've written in letters to you. But with the changes that have taken place here, I gave it up more or less because I thought it a forlorn hope. Anyway, pictures and story would have to be

cleared before publication but, if what they have in hand, *Life* or *Town & Country* want to go ahead, I'm game. Another Naval Intelligence Officer in Colombo told me I was crazy not to go ahead, as he has had several things accepted by magazines, and they were hungry for material and paid well. He also said the Navy Department approved of this sort of thing, when routed through the proper channels.

             NARRATOR (V.O.)
In the last week of September, Zimmermann was able to report that:

             ZIMMERMANN
Benjie Bromhead replied to my letter by telegram saying everything was in order for me to use the North-West Frontier Province pictures and story. How is the situation? Is anybody really interested or should it just be dropped? Curt Winsor also replied that he would get a release from the Navy Department.

BROMHEAD (V.O.) TELEGRAM [show it]
Peshawar   Lieutenant Albert Zimmermann   254 Ingle Road Karachi . . . Many thanks . . . your letter . . . that all right . . . go ahead . . . hope visit Karachi myself . . . next month . . . writing from Kashmir . . . Best wishes = Major Bromhead

             NARRATOR (V.O.)

The telegram in September 1944 was Zimmermann's last communication from Bromhead. However, in 2014, a woman recalled living in the North-West Frontier Province and later in England with the Bromhead family. She was the daughter of Mrs. Dorothea Leeper, who twice invited the Bromheads and Zimmermann for dinner in November 1943. After the Independence and Partition of India in 1947, Mrs. Leeper and her daughter returned to England. Mrs. Leeper worked as a secretary in London, and later remarried. In the meantime, her daughter lived until the age of nine at Thurlby Hall, and she shared a governess with the Bromhead children, who she called Diana-Jane, Anne and Johnny. She recalled growing up with them:

A WOMAN WHO KNEW THE BROMHEADS
[show Thurlby Hall images]
I lost touch with the Bromheads many, many, years ago but I am everlastingly grateful to them for taking me in.

NARRATOR (V.O.)
Barbara Zimmermann took what she thought were the best of the photos that her husband had taken in India to the National Geographic Society. She took photos of his trip along the North-West Frontier and others that he took on an intelligence mission, riding on a camel, in Baluchistan. And she offered to the *Geographic* the best of the photos that he took while walking

in the streets of Karachi and in Ceylon. The *National Geographic* purchased forty of the photographs, but never published them. The negatives were returned to Barbara, and she retained the right for her husband to use them. She also contacted *Reader's Digest*, but the *Digest* was not interested in the story. [pause] Barbara knew how to get things published, having grown up in a family that had been in business with the Lippincott publishing family in Philadelphia for several generations. And she had written articles that were published in both *Vogue* and the magazine of the *Garden Club of America*. It appears that most magazine publishers expected that India and the remote areas in Central Asia would be of little interest in America after the war was over. [pause] In 1950, Gordon Enders won second prize in the Army Short Story contest. His story, "The Nomad Woman," was published in *Collier's*. It is a beautiful narrative about the life of a rural couple in Afghanistan. This was probably his only post-war work of narrative writing:

ENDERS

The nomad woman came out of the low dark tent of goat's wool into the flaming sunset. She stooped over the newborn camel colt which sat on the ground nearby. A smile spread from the nomad woman's eyes, crinkling her russet cheeks and parting full lips over her white teeth. Gently, but with the sure touch of a woman with the very young, she ran her hands along the colt's firm back and deep shoulders. Her scarlet veil fell forward over the colt and the woman straightened up to toss her head and throw the cloth back. This made the dozens of coins which were sewn to her high-waisted gown jingle and ring. [pause] My jeep, my tribesman-driver, and I were guests of the nomad at their bivouac that evening, and there is nothing more admirable than the nomads' hospitality. The driver was a Pathan - an erect and vain youth from the Khyber Pass country with a veneer of modern polish. [pause] I sat on a blood-red rug spread over the desert stones and patted a great shepherd dog. Our host was an alert but single-minded man in his forties, wizened and dried by sun and weather. His spade-like beard was dyed bright red and he wore a green turban. (His red beard showed that he was a haj - that he had taken the pilgrimage to Mecca.) He was a descendant of the Prophet Mohammed, and well versed in the Koran. His name was Adam. He was of the clan of Suleiman, of the tribe of Ismail Khan. He called to his wife to hurry the food for his guests. She answered from inside the tent that the food was coming. Adam grunted and impatiently emptied the coals from his hookah on the bare ground.

"All our women and camels are beautiful. From Bokhara to Kandahar there are none finer! But, look you, sahib" - this to me - "Where can the camels graze; what will the women eat?" A great dam, built by Americans like myself, was soon to cover their highland pastures with deep water, to irrigate the crops of the settled tribes. He and I were unwillingly in opposing camps.

NARRATOR (V.O.)
In June 1950, the Korean War broke out, and Enders resumed his career in Army intelligence. He spent the next 12 years on active duty. He received the Legion of Merit for his service in Korea, and he rose to the rank of colonel. Gordon and Betty often traveled to spend time with his brother, Bob. In 2009, Bob's daughter recalled their visits as she spoke of her uncle Gordon and his wife Betty:

A NIECE OF GORDON ENDERS
Gordon was very kind to us. We called him "Uncle Bunkie." He was a great story teller. He once mentioned a trip that he took with two others - one was British - but he didn't say much about it. He didn't talk about his secret work. He was a good photographer and took a lot of pictures. I don't think any have been preserved. He did boast about being the first one in Afghanistan - the first military attaché, that is. Aunt Betty was

strict with us. She made us keep things neatly stored in our dresser drawers. I think she was twenty years older than Gordon, but he was devoted to her and he took care of her when she was in her final illness. My father was in the O.S.S., as a translator in Washington. He also didn't say much about his work, except that he didn't like Donovan, and that there was a lot of drinking in the O.S.S. My mother was very fond of Gordon. She introduced him to his second wife, who had previously been married to a professor at Swarthmore. She had a daughter with her first husband. Gordon was very fond of his step-daughter, especially, I think, because he and Betty didn't have any children of their own.

       NARRATOR
As a boy, A MAN WHO KNEW GORDON & BETTY ENDERS lived at Fort Meade, Maryland, with his parents. The headquarters of Army Intelligence and also the National Security Agency - NSA - are at Fort Meade. No one who lives at Fort Meade talks about their work, and no one asks anyone about what they are doing.

   A MAN WHO KNEW GORDON & BETTY
I remember Gordon Enders very well. He was a mysterious man, with a mysterious job. I understood that he worked for the government in some way. I thought that Gordon

once said he was a sergeant, but I doubted that. I think he was just pulling my leg. Gordon was very kind to his wife as she grew older, and Elizabeth - Mrs. Enders - was very kind to me, too. As a result of my experiences with him as a child, I have made a hobby of studying his career. I followed his trail from Ohio to France in World War I, and I located records of some of the units that he and his friends flew with. There is still much to learn about him. It's almost as if he intended his life to be mysterious.

    NARRATOR (V.O.)
Betty Enders died at the Fort Meade, Maryland, Army Hospital in 1962, shortly before Gordon retired. He moved to New Mexico after he married again, and he died there in 1978.

  A GREAT NIECE OF BETTY ENDERS
After Betty died, she was cremated. Her ashes were never interred, but they were placed in an urn that was kept by Gordon. Gordon's second wife was Elizabeth Garrahan, known as Liz. She died on a trip to Pennsylvania, and she was buried there beside her first husband. In 2017, I learned that her daughter, Nita Garrahan, had inherited the urn with Betty's ashes, and it was in her home in Albuquerque. I thought it would be good to have Betty's ashes interred beside Gordon in the Santa Fe National

Cemetery. The plan for inurnment of Betty's ashes was approved by Gordon's niece, who had baby-sat for Nita when she was a child. With her encouragement, Nita consented to have Betty's ashes placed beside Gordons's grave. I arranged for a tombstone with Betty's name, Elizabeth Ann Enders, to be placed next to Gordon's. His old stone was to be removed, with new language added to denote more about his service. My husband and I were present for the burial of Betty's ashes, and we placed flags beside each of the graves. Before we left, we also visited the grave of General Patrick Hurley, who Gordon had met in Kabul in 1944.

NARRATOR (V.O.)
Gordon's brother ROBERT ENDERS wrote his obituary for the College of Wooster:

ROBERT ENDERS
Gordon could read and speak Arabic, Persian, Urdu, and Hindi, as well as French, German, Mandarin, and Japanese. He returned to the U.S. from India in time to join the troops who went ashore at Okinawa and was underground in Korea when Japan surrendered. He carried the document of surrender of the Japanese commander in Korea to MacArthur. Only an old Wooster hand could have survived such a varied life.

NARRATOR (V.O.)
Zimmermann was officially appointed as Commanding Officer of the Naval Liaison Office in Karachi in the spring of 1944. As the war was progressing to a successful conclusion in Europe, he presided over a slowly diminishing staff of officers and enlisted personnel. He was sent back to America from Karachi in April 1945, to be trained for a new assignment. On his return to the U.S., he was found to be suffering from a peptic ulcer and was hospitalized. On V-J Day, Sunday, September 2, he was on convalescent leave with his family at their summer home on Long Island, New York. His daughter HELENE, known as Lanie, recalls that day:

HELENE (LANIE) ZIMMERMANN HILL
I'll never forget V-J Day. I was sixteen years old. It was a beautiful Sunday morning in Easthampton. We heard President Truman on the radio, saying that the war was finally over. It had been raining, but the rain stopped, the clouds parted, and a rainbow arched over the sky. [pause] Sometime during the war, my mother typed up a letter that Daddy wrote by hand in India. It described a trip that he took in northern India, in which he told about being the first to cross over a pass in a jeep. There was also a second letter about the trip. Both of these two letters were misplaced

after the war. My husband discovered a copy of the first one in my files in 2003, and he found the second letter in 2007 in the attic of my sister, Babs. Before she was married, Babs was in the C.I.A. in the Near East. She never talked about her undercover work, but she helped us to understand what Daddy was doing in India in World War II. My younger brother Warren was a career Foreign Service Officer. He was the acting Chief of Mission in Moscow, and then he was the last Ambassador to Yugoslavia. I think he may have known about Daddy's work in India, but he never spoke about it. Like Babs, he knew how to keep secrets. A NEIGHBOR, who lived next door to us in Haverford, was my best friend. Her father was a lieutenant in the Marines, and he was also in the O.S.S. He visited Daddy in Karachi, as he was heading somewhere further to the East. He was one of many who Daddy "called friends of Freeman" in his letters, and who stopped by to see him in Karachi. These men were all in the O.S.S. They were sent out by Daddy's friend Freeman Lincoln, who was a high-ranking O.S.S. officer in London at that time.

A NEIGHBOR

I never knew what Daddy did in the Marines or in the O.S.S. He never talked about it. My parents are buried in the cemetery of the Church of the Redeemer in Bryn

Mawr, Pennsylvania. There is no marker on either my father's tombstone or on Mr. Zimmermann's to show that either of them was in the service.

          NARRATOR (V.O.)
Albert Zimmermann was released from active duty at the end of December 1945, and he returned to his civilian career as a very successful wool broker and businessman. He remained in the Naval Reserve until he was promoted to lieutenant commander in 1946. He enjoyed a good life with his family and friends, and he was proud of his children's successes. He returned to his many hobbies, and he was especially good at golf. After playing 18 holes on a hot day in July 1961, he came home alone. He apparently had a cerebral hemorrhage - a stroke - from which he collapsed and died immediately.
[pause]
We might ask again some of the questions that were posed as this story began: Why were the three men sent on this trip along the Border? What was its purpose? What were they looking for? What did they find? Who ordered the trip? Who knew about it - before and after it was over? Was it kept secret intentionally, or was it just one of the many things that have been lost in the fog of war?
[pause]
Roderick Engert, son of the Minister to Afghanistan, said

without hesitation, when he was asked about the Trip in 2010:

          RODERICK ENGERT
"This trip was part of the Great Game."
          NARRATOR (V.O.)
Colonel "Tony" Streather, who was there in 1950, but had not heard of the Trip until 2010, said the same:

          STREATHER
"Yes, this Trip, it was all about the Great Game."

          NARRATOR (V.O.)
We haven't known about the Trip until now, nor have we remembered the lessons that the Three Men were taught as they went on the Trip. [pause]
A New Great Game has started. The Soviet Union invaded Afghanistan in 1979, and it withdrew without success in 1989. Osama bin-Laden was sheltered by the Taliban in Afghanistan, and from that base, he attacked the United States on September 11, 2001 – 9/11. We have now been at war in Afghanistan for 17 years. The Chinese and Pakistan and India and Afghanistan glare at each other across their borders in Central Asia. [pause]
As the saying goes, in French, *PLUS CA CHANGE, PLUS C'EST LA MEME CHOSE*. The more things change, the more they stay the same. [pause]
Is it now, as YOGI BERRA once said,

                    YOGI BERRA
               "De ja vu all over again"?

CUT TO:

IMAGE OF TIRICH MIR, WITH KIPLING'S WORDS PRINTED ACROSS
THE FACE OF THE MOUNTAIN. SLOWLY FADE TO DARKNESS.

                    NARRATOR (V.O.)
               Or as RUDYARD KIPLING said in 1900,
               in the words of the boy-spy, Kim,

                    RUDYARD KIPLING
               "The Game will never end until all
               the players are dead."

POST SCRIPT NOTES

Three Acts

There is no break in the Script, but there is a natural division in it, which divides it into three acts, as follows:

Act I - Prelude, with a climax when the Three Men meet in Peshawar, India, in November 1943, to start their trip along the Border of Afghanistan.

Act II, Part I - The Three Men ascend to the most remote place in India -- Chitral -- after crossing the Lowari Pass in a jeep. Their passage over the Lowari is the first-ever made in a motor vehicle. The climax of Act II, Part I, is when they return to Peshawar and speak with the Viceroy of India, Field Marshal Archibald Wavell. He had crossed the pass as a young officer on horseback, and he remembered how difficult it was.

Act II, Part II - The Three Men continue through very dangerous and hostile Tribal Territory (Waziristan) to Quetta, in Baluchistan. The climax of this Part is when they finally reach Quetta safely and are debriefed. They go on a picnic with the Governor and his family.

Act III - Aftermath, in which the Three Men go their separate ways, and the war ends. One of them, Gordon Enders, soon returns on two occasions to Afghanistan, and he then returns to the U.S. with malaria. The return trips of Enders to Kabul are interesting, but in Act III, there is a gradual denouement, without a climax.

The Voices

In approximate order of appearance

Those who are still alive are marked with an asterisk.
Others may still be alive but are not expected to appear.
They would be represented by actors (double asterisk).

Narrator

Sir Benjamin Bromhead, 5th Baronet Bromhead, OBE

Major Gordon Enders, AUS, Military Attaché, Kabul

Lieutenant Albert Zimmermann, USNR, Karachi

* A great-niece of Betty Enders

Betty Crump Enders, wife of Gordon Enders

Barbara Shoemaker Zimmermann, wife of Albert Zimmermann

Hon. Charles Thayer, U.S. Chargé d'affaires, Afghanistan

Lieutenant Curtin Winsor, USNR, Naval Intelligence Officer

John R. Harris, Esq., British Intelligence Officer, Karachi

* * Col. Anthony "Tony" Streather, OBE, mountaineer, soldier

Alghan Lusey, pre-war reporter in China; O.S.S. agent

* * Roderick Engert, son of Cornelius Engert; in O.S.S.

Hon. Cornelius van H. Engert, U.S. Minister to Afghanistan

Lady Nancy Bromhead, wife of Sir Benjamin Bromhead

* * A friend of the Bromhead family

* A niece of Gordon Enders

* A man who knew Gordon & Betty Enders

Robert Enders, brother of Gordon; in O.S.S. in Washington

* Helene Zimmermann Hill, daughter of Albert Zimmermann

* A next-door neighbor of the Zimmermanns

Yogi Berra, baseball player and wit

Rudyard Kipling, author of the book, *Kim*

"Three Men in a Jeep" Trailer Scenario

U.S. Army Major Gordon Enders, U.S. Navy Lieutenant Albert Zimmermann, and British Major Sir Benjamin Bromhead are ordered to depart from Peshawar, near the Khyber Pass, on what would seem to be a *Mission Impossible*: They are to take a jeep to Chitral, which is the most remote place in northwest India. Their road is only a narrow donkey trail. It runs along the side of a cliff, high above a tributary of the Kabul river, on the Border of India and Afghanistan. They would have to cross over the Lowari Pass, which had never before been traversed by a motor vehicle. It was late November, by which time the pass is usually closed because of snow and ice. On their return to Peshawar, they would report to the Viceroy of India. They would then continue for two more weeks along the Border, passing though the lawless, mountainous war zone of Waziristan, dodging bullets, bombs, and tank traps, to reach their final destination in the earthquake-devastated city of Quetta.

This mission was to allow Bromhead to deliver the annual British "tribute" of money to the hereditary rulers of the Pashtun tribes along the Border, in order to ensure the tribes' allegiance to Britain, and to keep peace between the tribes. The mission was also intended to show the two Americans the methods that were needed to defeat attempts by Russia to move south across Afghanistan and cross the Border into India. The Americans would thus be introduced to the "Great Game" that had gone on for more than two centuries in Central Asia between Britain and Russia. Looking ahead, some British colonial officials believed that after World War II ended, India would become independent, and the U.S. would take over British role in the Great Game with Russia.

Major Gordon Enders was a perfect spy. In his life and career, he was similar in many ways to Ernest Hemingway and John le Carré. Born in rural Iowa to a Presbyterian minister, he grew up in the Himalaya mountains on the border of India and Tibet. It was there that he learned of Rudyard Kipling's fictional boy-spy "Kim," and he dreamed, like Kim, of playing in the Great Game against Russia. He left college during World War I, and, like Hemingway, he drove an ambulance. He then became the pilot of reconnaissance planes, first for the French Foreign Legion, and then for the U.S. Army. He was grievously injured in a plane crash, but unlike Hemingway's nurse, Agnes von Kurowsky, played by Sandra Bullock, *In Love and War*, Enders' nurse married him, in her Red Cross uniform. Thus **Betty Crump Enders**, who was the beautiful daughter of a wealthy industrialist from New Jersey, became his partner. They traveled the world as fearless explorers, writers, and lecturers. He was darkly handsome, and he was always a spy. He became **Chiang Kai-shek**'s personal pilot, and he was a confidante of the **Panchan Lama**, ruler of Tibet. He spoke a dozen languages, but like le Carré, there was always some mystery about his life, and there were inconsistencies in what he wrote about it. He sometimes wore medals and decorations from four countries on his uniform. But he preferred to dress casually, in an aviator's sheep-lined leather bomber jacket, with a cigar clamped between his teeth, and a pistol holstered at his hip.

Lieutenant Albert Zimmermann was recruited into the business of spying before World War II in the same way that most Americans were recruited. He was independently wealthy, a graduate of an Ivy League college – the University of Pennsylvania – a member of a secret society – Sphynx – and he was a country club man who lived in an upscale suburb. He had many useful skills: he could sing while accompanying himself at the piano; he could chat and joke while playing a successful game of bridge; he was a champion golfer and better than average at tennis; and he was known to be a fine photographer with both a 35mm single-lens reflex camera and 16mm movie camera. He was handsome and unflappable, and he had a photogenic wife, **Barbara Shoemaker Zimmermann**. They had four lovely children. He could play a hidden game of spying as well as Cary Grant did in *Charade*. Indeed, Cary Grant himself once whispered in Barbara's ear as they were dancing on a cruise ship, "You are the most beautiful woman in this room." Most importantly, Al Zimmermann had four good friends who were close to **Vincent Astor**. Before he became president, **Franklin D. Roosevelt** had appointed his neighbor, Vincent Astor, to be the head of his informal intelligence operation, known as "The Room" in New York City. As president, FDR requested that the Navy appoint Commander Astor to vet all of the candidates for Naval

Intelligence on the East Coast, from Philadelphia to Boston. Zimmermann had taken still photos of the German Bund in Philadelphia for the FBI in 1936, and he secretly took movies of Nazi troops in Stuttgart in 1937. In 1942, Zimmermann was recruited as a Naval Intelligence Officer. In 1943 he was sent to Karachi, India, where he eventually became the Commanding Officer of the Naval Liaison Office. In this position, he was the chief of U.S. Naval Intelligence for what later became the four provinces of Pakistan.

British **Major Sir Benjamin Bromhead** was in civilian clothes when he met the two Americans in Peshawar in November 1943. He looked a bit like the quietly anonymous "George Smiley" in le Carré's *The Spy Who Came in from the Cold*, rather than Ian Fleming's "James Bond" – the lady-killer known as "007." Bromhead was casual, and not particularly handsome, unlike his great-uncle **Lieutenant Gonville Bromhead, VC**, the hero of the Battle of Rourke's Drift, who was played by Michael Caine in *Zulu*. Bromhead was a professional soldier, a graduate of Sandhurst, who was entitled to wear an array of medals, with clasps and oak leaf clusters, from campaigns in Iraq and Waziristan. He had recently been awarded the Order of the British Empire – the highly-prized "OBE." Sir Benjie wore lightly the honor of the hereditary 5th Baronet Bromhead of Thurlby Hall, Lincolnshire. It was a title that extended back to 1st Baronet, who was wounded and captured by the Americans in the Revolutionary War. Benjie spoke the dialects of the Pashtun tribes, and he knew their customs, known as *Pashtunwali*, which regulated all of their actions. Unlike the passionate and excitable officer played by Alec Guinness, in *Bridge over the River Kwai*, Sir Benjamin was as cool and calm in the face of danger as the British officers portrayed in *Dunkirk* and *Darkest Hour*.

Small parts are played by others who knew of the Trip, either as it was being planned or after it was over. And other interesting persons, too, are connected with them. Lieutenant **Curtin Winsor** was Zimmermann's classmate in Intelligence School and was later his point of contact in Washington at the Office of Naval Intelligence. He was married at that time to a former daughter-in-law of President Roosevelt, and he was thus the step-father of **FDR's grandson**. **Rex Benson**, the British Military Attaché in Washington, provided a card of introduction that Gordon Enders presented to the governor of the North-West Frontier Province in 1941. Benson was a cousin-in-law of **Sir Stuart Menzies**, head of MI-6 (and known as "M"); Menzies was the model for Ian Fleming's "C" in the James Bond novels. Benson was also a friend of the Prince of Wales, who became **King Edward VIII**, and of his paramour, **Wallis Simpson**; and of **Winston Churchill**. **Gene Markey**, Zimmermann's reporting senior as Chief of Naval Intelligence in India, led a double life before the war. He was a Naval Reserve Intelligence Officer; and a Hollywood producer who had married **Joan Bennett** and **Hedy Lamarr**. He produced the movie *Wee Willie Winkie*, starring **Shirley Temple**, which was fictionally set in the same area near Peshawar where the Three Men in a Jeep met to depart on their trip. During the war, he became a confidante of **Lord Mountbatten** in India, and after the war, he produced *In Harm's Way*, starring **John Wayne**. **Cornelius Engert** and his wife were well known to **Eleanor Roosevelt**, and his career was given a boost from her husband, FDR. It was a small world in those days, for Betty Enders and Eleanor Roosevelt were both on the Chautauqua Lecture Circuit, and so, too, was Gordon Enders.

THREE MEN IN A JEEP

By George Hill

A Documentary Film,
set in Central Asia in World War II

SCRIPT for TRAILER

FADE IN:

INSERT - A black screen, on which a small bright dot appears. It slowly enlarges to be seen as a revolving globe. The globe stops spinning and it is enlarged to focus on a map of Asia.

>   NARRATOR (V.O.)
>   Across Asia - from East to West -
>   there are many ranges of mountains
>   - known collectively as the
>   Himalayas.

The map fades to a diagram, showing the borders of China, India, Pakistan, Afghanistan, and the former Soviet republics, including Russia, Uzbekistan, and Tajikistan, as they are in 2018. The Himalayas are red-lined.

>   Some of the highest mountains in
>   the world are in the Himalayas -
>   Mount Everest, K-2, and Nanda Devi.

Red dots appear on the map to show each of these mountains, and map changes to names and borders of countries in 1943.

>   Further west is the range known as
>   the Hindu Kush, where the borders
>   of four countries meet at the
>   Wakhan Peninsula of Afghanistan. In
>   1943, only the narrow strip of the
>   Wakhan separated the Soviet Union
>   from India.

The borders of Chitral appear on the map, and a red dot for Tirich Mir mountain. Red-line the Hindu Kush range.

FADE IN: Image of Tirich Mir.

> The highest mountain in the Hindu Kush is Tirich Mir. Its south face towers over a small village, in a kingdom ruled for many centuries by the Mehtar of Chitral. It was the most remote place in British India in 1943.

"November 1943" appears on the image of Tirich Mir mountain.

> At the height of World War II, as the Allies were slowly advancing against their enemies in Europe and the Pacific, President Franklin Roosevelt and Prime Minister Winston Churchill planned to meet in Cairo, Egypt, with Chiang Kai-shek to discuss their next moves, and the future of the post-war world. In 1950, Churchill referred to this crucial moment as *The Hinge of Fate*.

The title words for the film, "Three Men in a Jeep" appear below "November 1943" across the image of Tirich Mir.

> And at the same time, three Allied military officers - two Americans and one an Englishman - were ordered to proceed to Chitral in an American jeep. Who were they? Why were they sent there? And what did they find?

DISSOLVE TO:
Image of Malakand, North-West Frontier Province, Political Agent's residence. A color painting of Malakand by Swayne-Thomas is shown, and several photos taken by

Zimmermann at Malakand. The photos show Enders' jeep, nicknamed "Ma Kabul." The Narrator introduces the THREE MEN. The men are in rough winter uniforms without insignia, stocking caps pulled down over their heads.

NARRATOR (V.O.)
The British officer is Major Sir Benjamin Bromhead. He is the 5th Baronet Bromhead, born in India and educated in England at Wellington College and the British military academy, Sandhurst. Bromhead is a career soldier. He is guiding the two Americans in this remote part of India. The Americans are Major Gordon Enders and Lieutenant Albert Zimmermann. Both of them are intelligence officers. Their business is spying. Enders is the Military Attaché in Kabul, Afghanistan. He has planned for many years to make this trip along the Afghan border. Zimmermann was sent to keep a close eye on Enders, and to keep a lookout for whatever may interest the Navy in this part of the world.

MAJOR SIR BENJAMIN BROMHEAD
I've just received a telegram from our political officer in Chitral. He says, "Ice, snow, and mud on Lowari Pass. Advise against any attempt to cross it." Gordon, What say you?

MAJOR GORDON ENDERS, U.S. ARMY
We'll make it, Benjie. Zimmermann?

                    LT AL ZIMMERMANN, U.S.N.R.
                    I'm game for it, too. Let's go.

                                                        CUT TO:
Image of three men in a jeep, on the summit of Lowari
Pass, from the cover of *Proceed to Peshawar*.

                                                        CUT TO:
Afghan music is played. Film of the three men at the
summit of Lowari Pass, accompanied by local militia and
hired men with horses. The jeep slides off of the road
several times, and it is pulled back by men with ropes. A
brief scene shows the men resting at a rough guest house
after crossing the pass. The film continues, with scenes
of Chitral: the palace of the Mehtar, men traipsing about
on foot, and on horseback on the field in front of Tirich
Mir.

                    NARRATOR (V.O.)
                    This wild country is where the game
                    called *bushkazi* is played. It is
                    the predecessor of the modern game
                    of polo. Teams of men on horses
                    compete against each other, to
                    throw the headless carcass of a
                    goat into a goal.

DISSOLVE TO:
Image of Thurlyby Hall, England. Montage of Saratoga,
Waterloo, India, Wellington College, Baronet's medal.

                    NARRATOR (V.O.)
                    In 1943, as a hereditary Baronet,
                    Sir Benjamin Bromhead, at age 43,
                    ranked highest in the social order
                    of the British Raj in the North-
                    West Frontier Province of India.
                    India was then the jewel of the
                    British Empire. Sir Benjie
                    believed, as did many in the
                    province, that India would become

free after the war. They thought that India would be partitioned, and that the North-West Frontier Province would become part of a new nation, Pakistan.

[pause]

Major Sir Benjamin was the 5th Baronet Bromhead of Thurlby Hall, Lincolnshire, England. His ancestors had been in military service in India for three generations. Long before, they had been prominent in England. The first baronet was wounded and captured at Saratoga in America in 1777, and the third baronet fought at the battle of Waterloo. Benjie's great-uncle, Lieutenant Gonville Bromhead, won the Victoria Cross at the Battle of Rourke's Drift in Africa, and was buried in Allahabad, India. Michael Caine played Gonville Bromhead in the movie *Zulu*. Benjie's father died when he was 10, and he thus succeeded to the baronetcy when his grandfather, the 4th baronet, died. Benjie was sent to England to be educated, and in 1914 he was a student at England's premier boarding school - Wellington College - when World War I broke out.

CUT TO:

MONTAGE - Images of John and Eva (Kellenbenz) Zimmermann, their home and his factories in Philadelphia, the Zimmermann family, and images of their children.

NARRATOR (V.O.)
Albert Zimmermann was the youngest of the three officers on this trip. At age 41, he was the most successful son of a poor immigrant who had achieved the American Dream. His father came to America as a young man, having been trained as a weaver by his father in Germany. In Philadelphia, his father invented new techniques of weaving and dyeing, and he eventually became a partner in Artloom, one of the largest carpet manufacturers in America. Al grew up in a grand house with servants near his father's factory. He attended public schools and the University of Pennsylvania, where he was president of the Glee Club. He was a member of Sphinx, a secret society. In 1917, after America entered World War I, one of Al's brothers was a soldier in the American Army in Europe. The father of Barbara Shoemaker, who Al later married, was also in Europe as the Chief of Ophthalmology for the American Expeditionary Forces. At age 15, Al knew about World War I, but he was not personally involved in it.

CUT TO:

MONTAGE - Images of the Enders family in Iowa, of Gordon Enders as a boy, file photos of rural Iowa in 1897, a passenger train in Chicago in about 1903, a passenger ship on the Atlantic at about that time, and docks in Philadelphia, Liverpool, and Calcutta, India, in about 1903.

                    NARRATOR (V.O.)
          Gordon Enders was the oldest of the
          three Allied officers who were
          poised to cross the Lowari pass
          into Chitral in November 1943. He
          called himself "an American Kim,"
          for the boy-spy who was the hero in
          Kipling's novel, *Kim*. He had long
          dreamed of making this trip, and he
          is said to have instigated it. He
          had acquired all of the skills
          necessary to do it. In October
          1941, he was sent to Kabul,
          Afghanistan, as the U.S. Military
          Attaché. In December 1941, shortly
          before Pearl Harbor was attacked,
          he crossed the Khyber Pass into
          Afghanistan. He was the first
          American diplomat to be stationed
          in Afghanistan. He came back
          across the Khyber Pass to meet the
          other two officers in Peshawar,
          India, at the start of this trip.
          Gordon Enders was born in rural
          Iowa in 1897. His father was a
          Presbyterian minister, and his
          mother was a teacher. Reverend
          Enders and his wife decided to go
          to India as missionaries in 1903.

MONTAGE - Images of the Enders family in India: group
picture of the family, and file photos of India in about
1903-1910, the mountain, Nanda Devi, and of Tibet, from
Enders' book, *Nowhere Else in the World*. Music continues
- Afghan, or Indian sitar.

                    NARRATOR (V.O.)
          The three Enders children - Miriam,
          Gordon, and Bob - would spend much

of their childhood in rural India. The family first lived at Etawah near the Grand Trunk Road. They then moved to Almorah, near the foot of the great sacred mountain, Nanda Devi.

Image of cover of the book, and then of Enders.

GORDON ENDERS

Almorah was one tiny unit in India's northern frontier line of defense, which stretched from Afghanistan to Burma. The situation to the north of Almorah was dangerous, where the forbidden and secretive land of Tibet was the focus of an imperialistic drama in which England, China and Russia were the principal actors. The first language I learned in India was the Hindustani of the plains, to which I soon added the Tibetan polyglot patois spoken in Almorah. Jowar Singh, a Hindu hillman, was our devoted mentor and teacher. But a far more important figure in turning my life toward its eventual goal was Jowar's father-in-law, a remarkable Tibetan named Chanti. I had read Kipling's *Kim*, and I recognized that Chanti's work was somehow a part of the British Intelligence Service. Some of his visitors were "Kim-men." The first Chinese I ever met was the trader, Wu Ming-fu, from Chengdu. Masih Ulla, was my Mohammaden friend, and from him I learned about the customs of the Muslims.

THREE MEN IN A JEEP

By George Hill

A Documentary Film,
set in Central Asia in World War II

POST SCRIPT NOTES

The Images

All of the images of the Zimmermann Family and of Zimmermann's World War II experiences are from the files of the Author

Other images are from Google Images and Internet searches

The 150 images of the Trip that are slowly scrolled down during V.O. by the Narrator and others from November 12 to December 12, 1943, were taken by Zimmermann. They can be dated from his photo log and from the record of the trip. Each was captioned by Zimmermann, and the captions will appear as subtitles. A few other photos, including the cover photo of *Proceed to Peshawar* (Naval Institute Press, 2013) were taken by Bromhead, and copies were given to Zimmermann.

Zimmermann's part is a composite of what he wrote in letters to his wife, and in his notes and typed reports. Details are in the 365 page privately-printed original draft of *Proceed to Peshawar* (copy available from the Author) and *Dearest Barb: From Karachi, 1943-1945* (Heritage Books, 2018).

The map of the area of the Trip, which is described on page 1 of this Script, can be visualized from the map shown in *Dearest Barb*, p. 221 (enlarged version on p. 337)[see below]. The unnamed principality of Chitral was reached by the Three Men in a Jeep after they crossed the Lowari Pass. Chitral is immediately south of what is now the Afghanistan-Pakistan border. Chitral extends along the southern border of the Wakhan Peninsula, which is the eastward extension of Afghanistan, south of the word "RUSSIA" on the map, to the border of China (not labeled on the map). The Wakhan Peninsula lies between what are now the countries of Tajikistan on the north (marked RUSSIA on the map) and Pakistan on the south. Tirich Mir, the highest mountain in the Hindu Kush range, is in Chitral. On the map, Tirich Mir is located just south of the small upward hook that marks the boundary of the Wakhan Peninsula. It is south of the words "R. Oxus" at the entrance to the peninsula.

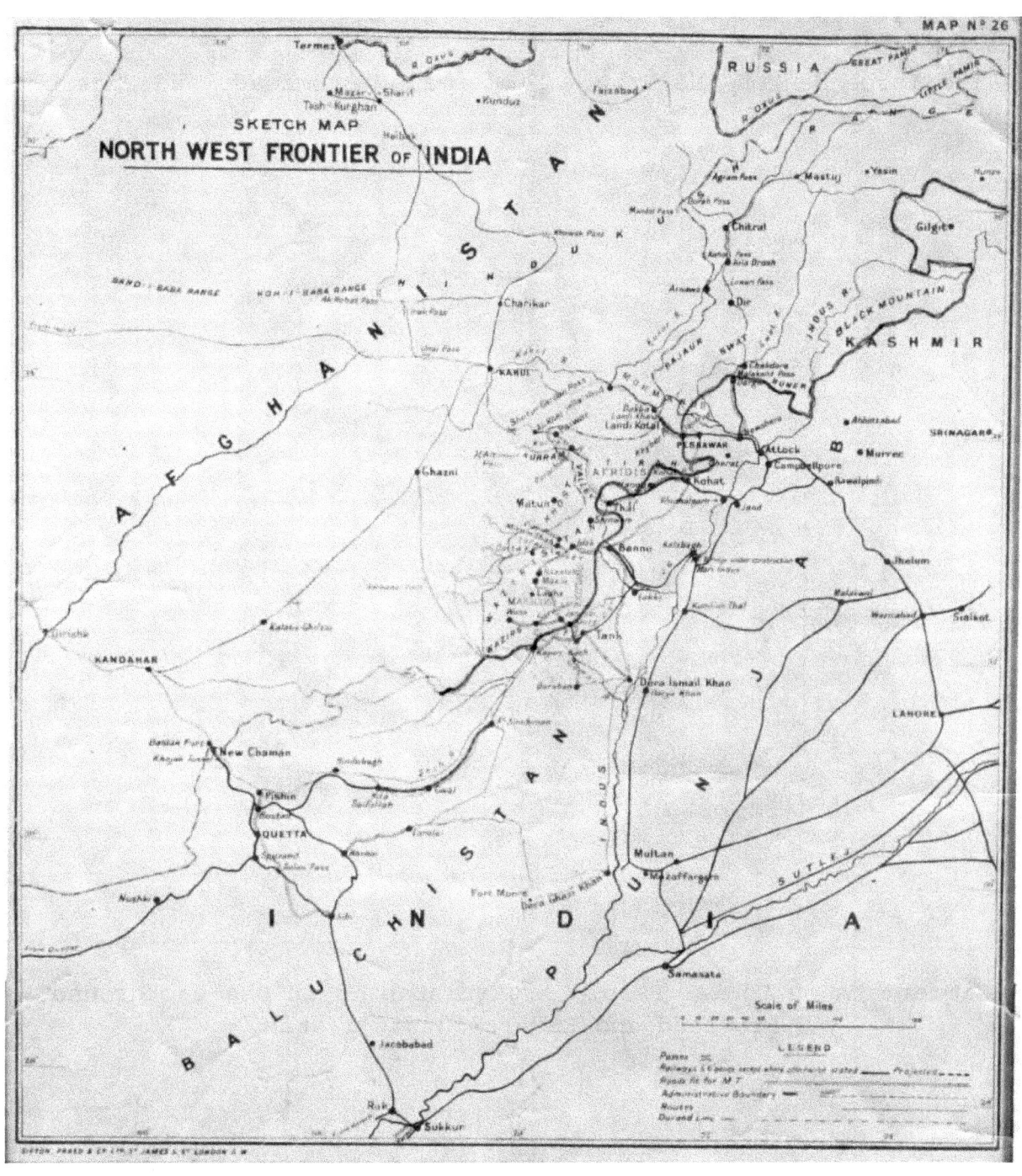

A Sample of Images for Three Men in a Jeep

The Three Men on the Trip - Zimmermann, Bromhead, and Enders

Zimmermann on Lowari Pass. Afghanistan is in the background.
Bromhead and Enders in Waziristan.

Albert Zimmermann

Barbara Zimmermann

The Bromhead Estate

Thurlby Hall, Lincolnshire
Seat of the Bromheads

Michael Caine as Lt. Gonville Bromhead
In the movie, *Zulu*

Gordon Enders and Elizabeth "Betty" Crump Enders

1919

With his "Golden Passport" from Tibet

Betty Enders in 1919 and as a Lecturer

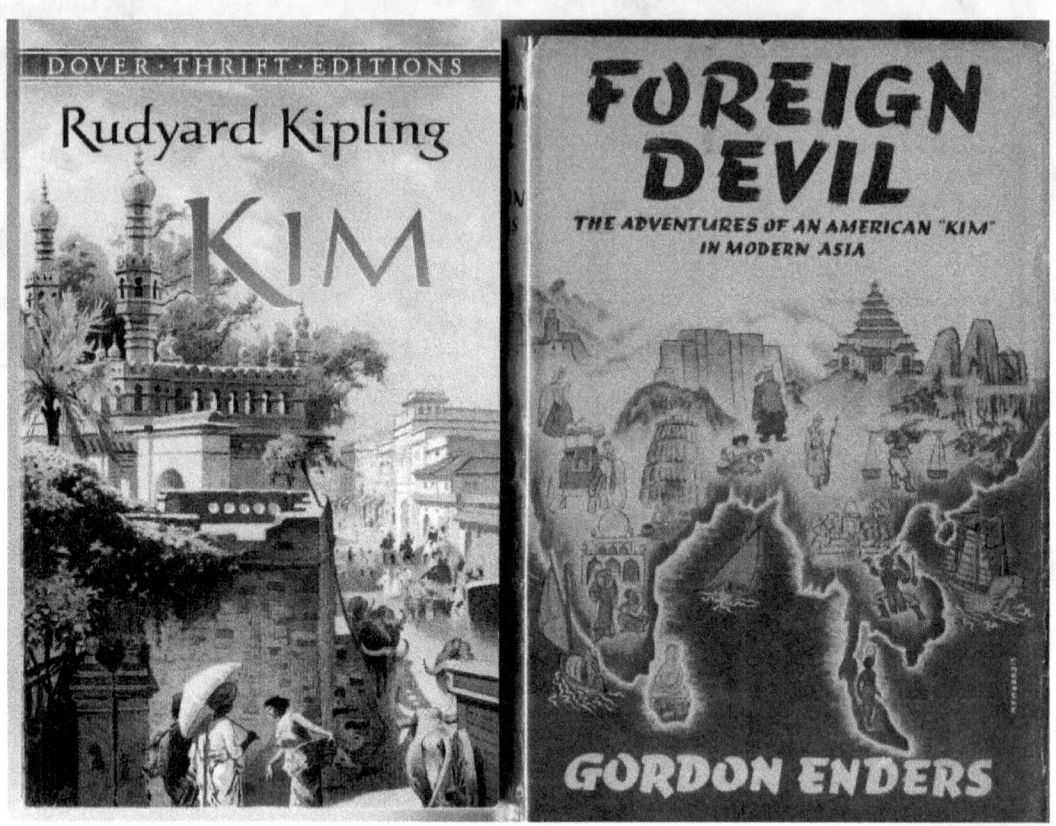

Enders patterned his own life after the boy spy, Kim,
In Kipling's novel, *Kim*.

Nanda Devi, on the border of India and Tibet

Tirich Mir, in the Hindu Kush - Pakistan

Still Shots from Zimmermann's 16-millimeter Movies

Surreptitious movie taken of Nazi troops marching in Stuttgart, 1937

The Zimmermanns' maid, Anna, and her husband, Paul, in Stuttgart, 1937 (L)
Their marriage in Philadelphia in 1936 was photographed for the FBI by Albert Zimmermann
(see *"Dearest Barb" from Karachi*, p. 7)
They were ardent supporters of the Third Reich

Major Gordon Enders, USA, on Lowari Pass, with Chitrali Scout – 18 November 1943

The Jeep, "Ma Kabul" – Major Enders being pulled back onto the road, north of Lowari Pass

Major Enders at Drosh Levy Post, north of Lowari Pass – 19 November 1943

Palace of the Mehtar of Chitral – 20 November 1943

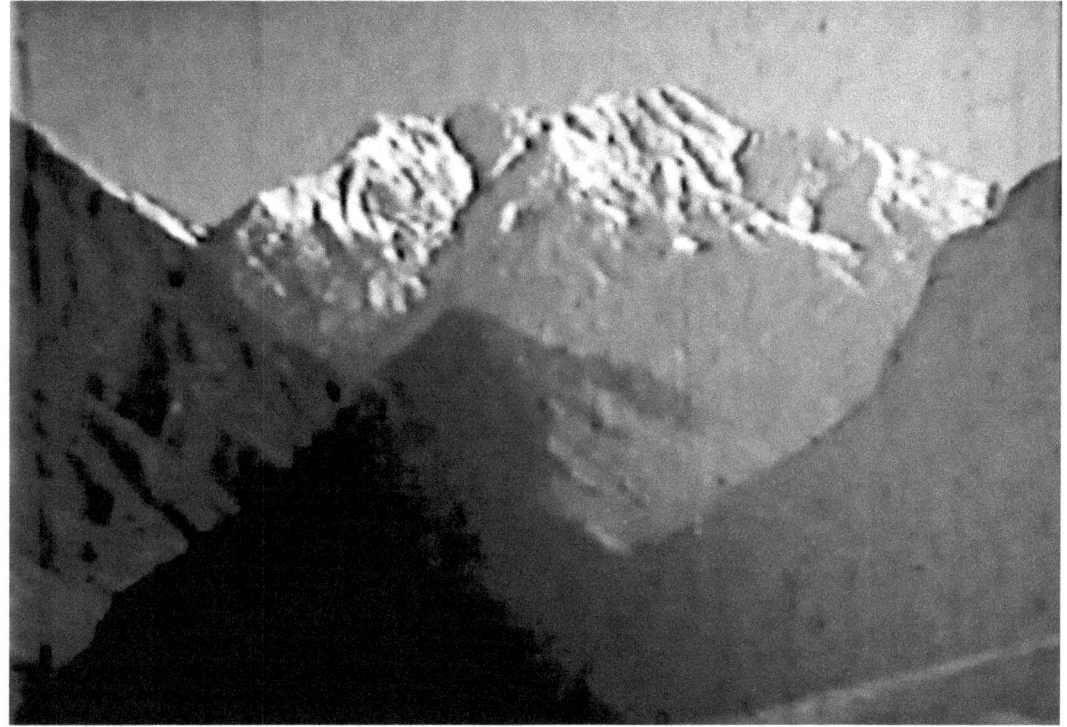

Tirich Mir – South Face – Highest Peak in the Hindu Kush Range
From Chitral Village – 21 November 1943 – First known movie taken of Tirich Mir

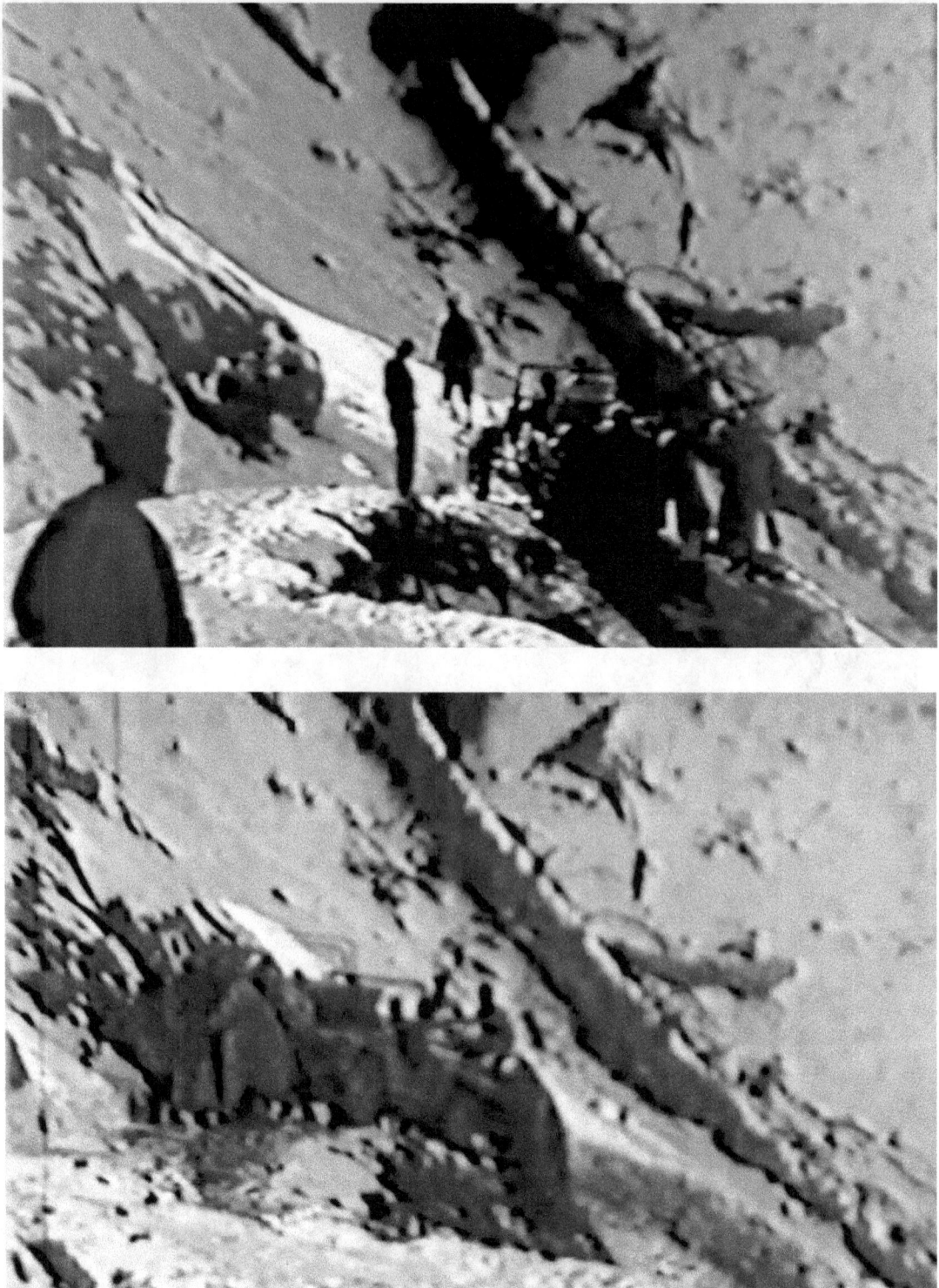

Major Enders in "Ma Kabul" being pulled back on the road to Lowari – 20 November 1943

Parade of Indian Army troops, North-West Frontier Province – November 1943

Governor's picnic lunch during *chikor* (partridge) shoot, near Quetta, Baluchistan – 11 December 1943
Enders is partially hidden on the left, the Governor is leaning forward beside him

Zimmermann also took many movies in Karachi
and elsewhere in India and Ceylon

Mahan Kishin, Zimmermann's head "bearer" in Karachi,
with the Naval Liaison Office in the background

Acknowledgements

I would like to thank my wife's parents, Albert and Barbara (née Shoemaker) Zimmermann, for saving the World War II records of Al's service in the Navy in India, including letters, movies, photographs, and his other papers. And thanks to their elder daughter, Barbara (née Zimmermann) Johnson, for preserving these records and helping to interpret them

Thanks to Richard Latture, editor of *Naval History*, for provisionally accepting the story of the Trip as I first attempted to present it. And thanks to *Appalachia* for first publishing the story in 2008, as "An audacious World War II trek," and thus encouraging me to continue. And to Maynard Creel, who read the *Appalachia* article and thus discovered our mutual interest in Gordon Enders. To Patty Hoenigman, who with Maynard's help, discovered our mutual interest in her great-aunt, Betty (née Crump) Enders. And thanks to Dr. Gertrude "Trudy" (née Enders) Huntington for helping me to understand the Enders family.

I appreciate the thoughtful help of Richard "Rick" Russell, who accepted *Proceed to Peshawar* by the U.S. Naval Institute Press, and then guided the staff of the Press in the revision needed for publication.

Thanks to Romilly Leeper for reading *Proceed to Peshawar,* and for her gentle correction of her family's name; and then for her memories of the Bromhead family. And to Col. Anthony "Tony" Streather, OBE, for his recollections of the North-West Frontier Province, and Roderick Engert for his remembrances of Afghanistan in World War II.

I thank Harvey Rochman for discovering *Proceed to Peshawar* and encouraging me to make a movie about it. He suggested making it as a semi-fictional film *Khyber Pass*, focused on the life of Gordon Enders. Rick Russell responded quickly with assistance in making a movie by introducing me to the Naval Institute Press's Agent, Steven Moore of the Kohner Agency, and by offering candid advice about the movie business. Steven suggested Michael Morales, Esq., and he became my very useful Hollywood lawyer. Harvey introduced me to many who helped form the idea for *Khyber Pass* as a movie, including especially Ed Asner, Kevin Connor, Howard Kazanjian, Galen Walker, Ian Merrick, Jonathan Sanger, Ken Atchity, Norman Stephens, Michael Mercier, and Pius Savage.

Two Script writers, Antonia "Toni" Nagy and Joe Verrastro, brought *Khyber Pass* to the attention of many actors, directors, producers, and advisors, who saw its potential, even though it didn't achieve enough funding to become a movie. Toni's father, Professor Gregory Nagy, was also supportive and helpful, too. I appreciate the time and effort spent by Dr. Frank Kwong on this project, and also suggestions by the staff in Baltimore at Johns Hopkins University-Maryland Institute College of Art (JHU-MICA), especially Will Bryson. I appreciate the offers by Rob Cole and Rod Lopez to work with me on the Trailer Script.

Warm thanks to the staff of Heritage Books: Publications Division Director, Leslie Wolfinger; and Editor, Debbie Riley.

And most of all, thanks to my family – to my daughters Sarah and Lana, and especially to my wife, Lanie.

Bibliography
Sources, Registrations, and Suggested Reading

[Aldrich] "Malcolm Aldrich, 86; Headed a Foundation. Obituary, *New York Times* (3 August 1986).

Atchity, Kenneth. *Sell Your Story to Hollywood: Writer's Pocket Guide to the Business of Show Business.* Los Angeles: Story Merchant Books, 2016.

[Benson] "Sir Rex Benson, Banker, 79, Dies: Was Military Attaché Here from 1941 to 1944" *New York Times* (28 September 1968).

Brown, Anthony Cave. *The Last Hero: Wild Bill Donovan.* New York City: Vintage Books/Random House, 1982.

_____. *The Secret Servant: The Life of Sir Stewart Menzies. Churchill's Spymaster.* London: Michael Joseph, Published by the Penguin Group, [1987] 1988.

Buhite, Russell D. *Patrick J. Hurley and American Foreign Policy.* Ithaca: Cornell University Press, 1973.

Churchill, Sir Winston. *The Story of the Malakand Field Force: An Episode of Frontier War.* Seven Treasures Publications, 2009 [Churchill, Winston. *Malakand Field Force.* London: Longmans, Green and Co., 1898].

_____. *The Second World War.* 5 vols. Vol. 4: *The Hinge of Fate.* Vol. 5: *Closing the Ring.* Boston, Mass.: Houghton Mifflin Company, 1981.

Courcy, Anne de. *The Viceroy's Daughters: The Lives of the Curzon Sisters.* New York City, N.Y.: HarperCollins/Perennial, [2000] 2002.

Crile, George. *Charlie Wilson's War: The Extraordinary Story of How the Wildest Man in Congress and a Rouge CIA Agent Changed the History of Our Times.* New York City, N.Y.: Grove Press, 2003.

Curzon, George N. *Persia and the Persian Question.* London: Frank Cass & Co., Ltd. [1892] 1966. 2 vols.

_____. *The Pamirs and the Source of the Oxus.* London: The Royal Geographical Society, 1896.

_____. *Russia in Central Asia in 1889 and the Anglo-Russian Question* (London: Frank Cass & Co., Ltd [1889] 1967.

Cutting, Suydam. *The Fire Ox and Other Years.* New York City, N.Y.: Charles Scribner's Sons, 1940.

_____. "Cheetah Hunting," pp. 167-172, in Plimpton, George (ed. and Introduction). *As Told at the Explorers Club: More Than Fifty Gripping Tales of Adventure*. Guilford, Conn.: The Lyons Press / Globe Pequot Press, [2003] 2005.

Dorril, Stephen. *MI6: Inside the Covert World of Her Majesty's Secret Intelligence Service*. New York City, N.Y.: Simon & Schuster/A Touchstone Book, [2000] 2002.

Dorwart, Jeffery M. *Conflict of Duty: The U.S. Navy's Intelligence Dilemma, 1919-1945.* Annapolis, Md.: Naval Institute Press, 1983.

Enders, Elizabeth Crump. "How to Sell More Goods to Colleges and Schools." *Dry Goods Economist* 74 (28 February 1920), 49, 51, 53.

_____. "Why the Wanamaker Catalogue Is Managed by a Woman: Miss Clara Bogart Has Found Mail-Order Success by Combining Advertising with Merchandising Judgment." *Printer's Ink Monthly* 1 (1921), 19-20.

_____. *Swinging Lanterns.* New York, N.Y.: D. Appleton and Company, 1923.

_____. *Temple Bells and Silver Sails.* New York, N.Y.: D. Appleton and Company, 1925.

_____. "Three Vignettes: Women in the East." *Journal of the American Asiatic Association* (June 1934): 386-8.

_____. "East Meets West in Japan's Women." *Independent Woman.* 15-16 (April 1936): 102-4, 130.

Enders, Gordon Bandy, and Edward Anthony. *Nowhere Else in the World.* New York: Farrar & Rinehart, 1935.

Enders, Gordon Bandy. F*oreign Devil: An American Kim in Modern Asia.* New York: Simon and Schuster, 1942.

_____. "Prohibition in Old India" (with decoration by Herb Roth). *Asia: The American Magazine on the Orient* 20 (No. 10, November 1920): 1003-4.

_____. "The Last Theocrat: The Panchan Lama of Tibet." *World Youth* (30 November 1935), 7. Copy in Patrick J. Hurley Collection, Western History Collection, Oklahoma University Libraries, Box 493C, Folder 4. With photo of the Panchan Lama.

_____. "Night Raiders in China." *Liberty* (3, 17, 31 July 1937).

[Enders] Anon., "Flying Gold Out of Tibet: Planes Invade Land of the Lamas." *Modern Mechanix Hobbies Inventions* (November 1936), 76-7, 120.

_____. "The Nomad Woman." *Collier's* (7 October 1950): 16, 62.

[Enders, Gordon B.] Hoy, William. "A Yankee Adventurer and the 'Living Buddha'." *Chinese Digest* (28 February 1936), 11, 14.

_____. Find A Grave. Gordon Bandy Edwards. Birth May 7, 1897. Death Sept. 2, 1978.

_____. Gordon B. Enders, Obituary. "Former Adviser to Chiang Dies." *Albuquerque Journal* (September 1978).

Engert, Jane Morrison. *Tales from the Embassy: The Extraordinary World of C. Van H. Engert.* Westminster, Md.: Heritage Books/Eagle Editions, 2006.

Ewans, Sir Martin. *Afghanistan: A Short History of Its People and Politics.* New York: Perennial/HarperCollinsPublishers, (2001) 2002.

Filkins, Dexter. *The Forever War.* New York: Alfred A. Knopf, Borzoi Books, 2008.

Fox, Ernest F. *Travels in Afghanistan.* New York, N.Y.: The Macmillan Company, 1943.

_____. *By Compass Alone.* Philadelphia, Pa: Dorrance & Company, 1971.

Hill, George J. *Proceed to Peshawar: The Story of a U.S. Navy Intelligence Mission on the Afghan Border, 1943.* Annapolis: Naval Institute Press, 2013.

_____. *American Dreams: Ancestors and Descendants of John Zimmermann and Eva Katherine Kellenbenz, Who Were Married in Philadelphia in 1885.* Berwyn Heights, Md.: Heritage Books, 2016.

_____. *"Dearest Barb" from Karachi, 1943-1945: Letters and Photographs in the World War II Papers of a Naval Intelligence Officer, Lieutenant Albert Zimmermann, USNR.* Berwyn Heights, Md.: Heritage Books, 2016.

Hill, George J. and Helene Z. Hill. "An audacious World War II trek: Three allied officers traverse the Lowari Pass to Chitral in 1943. The southern route to Tirish Mir and Hindu Kush Mountains." *Appalachia: Journal of the Appalachian Mountain Club* 49 (no. 2, Summer/Fall 2008): 64-75.

Hopkirk, Peter. *Trespassers on the Roof of the World: The Secret Exploration of Tibet.* [1982] New York: Kodansha International, 1995.

_____. *The Great Game: The Struggle for Empire in Central Asia.* New York, N.Y.: Kodansha Globe, 1992.

_____. *Setting the East Ablaze: Lenin's Dream of an Empire in Asia.* [1984] New York, N.Y.: Kodansha International, Inc., 1995.

_____. *Quest for Kim: In Search of Kipling's Great Game.* [1996] Ann Arbor, Mich.: University of Michigan Press, 1999.

Hyde, H. Montgomery. *Room 3603: The Incredible True Story of Secret Intelligence Operations During World War II.* New York City, N.Y.: The Lyons Press, [1962] 2001. Foreword by Ian Fleming.

Jeffery, Keith. *The Secret History of MI6.* New York City, N.Y.: The Penguin Press, 2010.

Lohbeck, Don. *Patrick J. Hurley.* Chicago: Henry Regnery Company, 1956.

Kipling, Rudyard. *The Writings in Prose and Verse of Rudyard Kipling.* New York: Charles Scribner's Sons, 1897-8. 12 vols.

_____. *Kipling Stories: Twenty-eight Exciting Tales by the Master Storyteller.* New York City, N.Y.: Platt & Munk, 1960.

_____. *Kim.* [1901] Mineola, N.Y.: Dover Publications, Inc., 2005.

Markey, Gene. *His Majesty's Pyjamas.* New York, N.Y.: Covici-Friede-Publishers, 1934.

_____. *Women, Women, Everywhere.* New York, N.Y.: Bobbs-Merrill, 1964.

Meyer, Karl Ernest, and Shareen Blair Brysac. *Tournament of Shadows: The Great Game and the Race for Empire in Central Asia.* New York: Basic Books, 1999.

Miles, Milton E. *A Different Kind of War: The Unknown Story of the U.S. Navy's Guerilla Forces in World War II China.* Garden City, N.Y: Doubleday & Co., 1967.

Mitchell, Norval. *Sir George Cunningham: A Memoir.* Blackwood, 1968.

Persico, Joseph. *Roosevelt's Secret War: FDR and World War II Espionage.* New York City, N.Y.: Random House, 2002.

Rhodes, Richard. *Hedy's Folly: The Life and Breakthrough Inventions of Hedy Lamarr, the Most Beautiful Woman in the World.* New York, N.Y.: Doubleday, 2011.

Smith, Richard Harris. *OSS: The Secret History of America's First Central Intelligence Agency.* Guilford, Conn.: The Lyons Press, an imprint of The Globe Pequot Press, [1972] 2005.

Sanger, Jonathan. *Making the Elephant Man: A Producer's Memoir.* Jefferson, NC: MacFarland & Co., 2016.

Snyder, Blake. *Save the Cat: The Last Book on Screenwriting You'll Ever Need.* Studio City, Calif.: Michael Wiese Productions, 2005.

[Streather, Anthony] In "Friends Who Died at the Top" *[London] The Sunday Times* (2 September 2007).

Swayne-Thomas, April. *Indian Summer: A Mem-sahib in India and Sind.* London: New English Library, Barnard's Inn, Holborn, 1981.

Thayer, Charles W. *Bears in the Caviar.* Philadelphia, Penna.: J. B. Lippincott Co., [1950] 1951.

_____. *Hands Across the Caviar.* Philadelphia, Penna.: J. B. Lippincott Company, 1952.

_____. *Diplomat.* New York City, N.Y.: Harper & Brothers, 1959.

_____. *Guerrilla.* New York City, N.Y.: Harper & Row, 1963.

Thomas, Lowell. *Beyond Khyber Pass into Forbidden Afghanistan.* New York City, N.Y.: Grosset & Dunlap, by arrangement with The Century Company, revised ed., 1925. Illustrated with photographs by Harry A. Chase, F.R.G.S. and the author.

Tolstoy, Ilya. "Across Tibet from India to China." *National Geographic* 90 (August 1946), 169-222

Tung, Rosemary Jones. *A Portrait of Lost Tibet.* New York, N.Y.: Holt, Rinehart and Winston, 1980. The story of the Tolstoy/Dolan mission and Dolan's unpublished papers, illustrated with some of their 2000 black and white photos.

Wake, Jehanne. *Kleinwort Benson: The History of Two Families in Banking.* Oxford: Oxford University Press, 1997.

_____. "Benson, Sir Reginald Lindsay [Rex] (1889-1968)," in *Dictionary of National Biography*. Vol. 5. (Oxford: Oxford University Press, 2004), 194-6.

[Wavell] Connell, John. *Wavell: Scholar and Soldier, to June 1941.* London: Collins, 1964.

_____ Fort, Adrian. *Archibald Wavell: The Life and Times of an Imperial Servant.* London: Jonathan Cape, 2009.

_____ Lewin, Ronald. *The Chief: Field Marshal Lord Wavell, Commander-in-Chief and Viceroy, 1939-1947.* New York City, N.Y.: Farrar, Straus and Giroux, 1980.

World War 1 US AIR SERV RL1: The US Air Service in World War 1: https://media.defense.gov/2010. Also see Google Images for World War 1 US AIR SERV RL1.

Yu, Maochun. *OSS in China: Prelude to Cold War.* New Haven, Conn.: Yale University Press, 1997.

Zimmermann, Barbara S. "This War – And Brave Little Women." *Vogue* (1 March 1944), 137, 140.

_____. *Mutterings.* Wynnewood, Pa.: Livingston Publishing Co., 1969.

Registrations

Khyber Pass. Writers Guild of America-West, Movie Registration Number 1828189. 3/3/2016

Khyber Pass. Copyright Registration Case Number: 1-4391825841. Application Format: Standard Case. Type: Work of the Performing Arts. Contact Name: Michael Morales. Opened: 1/30/2017. For Khyber Pass Productions, LLC (George J. Hill, owner).

Khyber Pass – Revision. WGA-W, Movie Registration Number 1915138. 9/26/2017

Three Men in a Jeep. Trailer Script. Copyright Registration Case Number: 1-6758468091. Application Format: Standard Case. Type: Work of the Performing Arts. Contact Name: George Hill. Opened 7/11/2018.

Three Men in a Jeep. Script. Copyright Registration Case Number 1-6761552871. Application Format: Standard Case. Type: Work of the Performing Arts. Contact Name: George Hill. Opened 13 July 2018.

Other Books by the Author

Leprosy in Five Young Men
Outpatient Surgery (3 editions)
Clinical Oncology, with John Horton
Edison's Environment (2 editions)
Intimate Relationships: Church and State in the U.S. and Liberia (2 editions)
Proceed to Peshawar

© JanPressPhotomedia

GEORGE J. HILL, M.D., M.A., D.Litt., is a Professor Emeritus at the New Jersey Medical School, Rutgers University. A fifth-generation Iowan, he was born in Cedar Rapids and graduated from high school in Sac City, where he became an Eagle Scout and received the Bausch and Lomb Science Award, the National Thespian Award, and was a member of the Iowa State prize-winning percussion ensemble and two-mile relay team. In 2001, he was placed on his high school's Honor Roll of Graduates.

Dr. Hill attended Yale College, where he graduated with High Honors in history, and Harvard Medical School, on scholarships, while working part time at many jobs: as a ranch hand, cub reporter, salesman, lab tech, and science teacher at a junior college. He then began a 40-year career as a surgeon, scientist, and medical school professor. He wrote prize-winning books and papers on subjects as diverse as leprosy, malaria, toxicology, public health, cancer, and surgery. He served as chairman of advisory panels for the U.S. government, many professional societies, the American Cancer Society, Boy Scouts of America, the Y.M.C.A., and the American Red Cross. He was elected as a Fellow of the Royal Society of Medicine, the American College of Surgeons, and the Explorers Club.

After retiring from surgery and oncology, he continued to work as a historian, author, genealogist, and popular lecturer. He received an M.A. in history from Rutgers University and a D.Litt. from Drew University. He has also travelled with his wife and family to more than 50 countries and they have trekked on all seven continents. He had a simultaneous career in U.S. military service, beginning in 1950, when he volunteered for the U.S. Marine Corps. He became a military parachutist, and he retired as a Navy Reserve Medical Corps captain in 1992, having been on active duty in four wars: the Korean War; the Cuban Missile Crisis of the Cold War; the Viet Nam War; and the First Gulf War. His Reserve service included duty in the Navy Command Center at the Pentagon as Chief of the Contingency Planning Branch of U.S. Navy Medicine. His many awards and decorations include the Navy Meritorious Service Medal, the Gorgas Medal, the New Jersey Distinguished Service Medal, the Outstanding Service Medal of the Uniformed Services University; and as a civilian, the St. George Medal of the American Cancer Society and the Distinguished Eagle Scout Award.

In 2006, he was invited to give the keynote address for the annual Navy Birthday celebration at the National Reconnaissance Office. He spoke to the NRO about the fictional Doctor Stephen Maturin in Patrick O'Brian's novels about Jack Aubrey and warfare at sea at the end of the eighteenth century. The title of his lecture was "Master and Commander, Surgeon and Spy." His book, *Proceed to Peshawar*, won a Finalist's Medal at the Indie Book Awards festival in 2015.

www.ingramcontent.com/pod-product-compliance
Lightning Source LLC
Chambersburg PA
CBHW080248170426
43192CB00014BA/2597